Roland G. Meinert
John T. Pardeck
John W. Murphy
Editors

Postmodernism, Religion and the Future of Social Work

Postmodernism, Religion and the Future of Social Work has been co-published simultaneously as *Social Thought*, Volume 18, Number 3 1998.

Pre-publication
REVIEWS,
COMMENTARIES,
EVALUATIONS . . .

"**P**ostmodernism, Religion and the Future of Social Work* tackles not only the difficult questions surrounding post-modernism but also how it impacts upon religion and social work. Bringing together postmodernism, religion, and the future of social work was an ambitious project. Despite this complex charge, Meinert, Pardeck, Murphy and the excellent group of authors they assembled managed to beautifully execute this difficult project. *Postmodernism, Religion and the Future of Social Work* is an important book for all those who ponder the future of social work and religion in a postmodern age."

Howard Jacob Karger, PhD
Professor and Doctorate Program Director,
Graduate School of Social Work
University of Houston

Postmodernism, Religion and the Future of Social Work

Postmodernism, Religion and the Future of Social Work has been co-published simultaneously as *Social Thought*, Volume 18, Number 3 1998.

The *Social Thought* Monographs/"Separates"

Spirituality in Social Work: New Directions, edited by Edward R. Canda

Postmodernism, Religion and the Future of Social Work,
edited by Roland G. Meinert, John T. Pardeck, and John W. Murphy

These books were published simultaneously as special thematic issues of *Social Thought* and are available bound separately. Visit Haworth's website at http://www.haworth.com to search our online catalog for complete tables of contents and ordering information for these and other publications. Or call 1-800-HAWORTH (outside US/Canada: 607-722-5857), Fax: 1-800-895-0582 (outside US/Canada: 607-771-0012), or e-mail: getinfo@haworth.com

Postmodernism, Religion and the Future of Social Work

Roland G. Meinert
John T. Pardeck
John W. Murphy
Editors

Postmodernism, Religion and the Future of Social Work has been co-published simultaneously as *Social Thought,* Volume 18, Number 3 1998.

The Haworth Pastoral Press
An Imprint of
The Haworth Press, Inc.
New York • London

3604879971

Published by

The Haworth Pastoral Press, 10 Alice Street, Binghamton, NY 13904-1580 USA

The Haworth Pastoral Press is an imprint of The Haworth Press, Inc., 10 Alice Street, Bing-hamton, Ny 13904-1580 USA.

Postmodernism, Religion and the Future of Social Work has been co-published simultaneously as *Social Thought,* Volume 18, Number 3 1998.

Cover design by Thomas J. Mayshock Jr.

Library of Congress Cataloging-in-Publication Data

Postmodernism, religion and the future of social work / Roland G. Meinert, John T. Pardeck, John W. Murphy, editors.
    p. cm.
    "Has been co-published simultaneously as Social thought, Volume 18, Number 3 1998."
    Includes bibliographical references and index.
    ISBN 0-7890-0516-6
    1. Social service–Philosophy. 2. Public welfare–Philosophy. 3. Postmodernism. 4. Postmod-ernism–Religious aspects. I. Meinert, Roland G. II. Pardeck, John T. III. Murphy, John W. IV. Social thought.
HV40.P66 1998
361'.001–dc21   98-16142
                                                                                                              CIP

INDEXING & ABSTRACTING

Contributions to this publication are selectively indexed or abstracted in print, electronic, online, or CD-ROM version(s) of the reference tools and information services listed below. This list is current as of the copyright date of this publication. See the end of this section for additional notes.

- *Abstracts of Research in Pastoral Care & Counseling,* Loyola College, 7135 Minstrel Way, Suite 101, Columbia, MD 21045
- *Applied Social Sciences Index & Abstracts (ASSZA) (Online: ASSI via Data-Star) (CDRom: ASSIA Plus),* Bowker-Sauer Limited, Maypole House, Maypole Road, East Grinstead, West Sussex, RH191HH, England
- *caredata CD: the social and community care database,* National Institute for Social Work, 5 Tavistock Place, London WC1H 9SS, England
- *CNPIEC Reference Guide: Chinese National Directory of Foreign Periodicals,* P.O. Box 88, Beijing, People's Republic of China
- *IBZ International Bibliography of Periodical Literature,* Zeller Verlag GmbH & Co., P.O.B. 1949, d-49009 Osnabruck, Germany
- *INTERNET ACCESS (& additional networks) Bulletin Board for Libraries ("BUBL") coverage of information resources on INTERNET, JANET, and other networks.*
  - <URL:http://bubl.ac.uk/>
  - The new locations will be found under <URL:http://bubl.ac.uk/link/>.
  - Any existing BUBL users who have problems finding information on the new service should contact the BUBL help line by sending e-mail to <bubl@bubl.ac.uk>.
  The Andersonian Library, Curran Building, 101 St. James Road, Glasgow G4 0NS, Scotland
- *National Periodical Library,* Guide to Social Science & Religion, P. O. Box 3278, Clearwater, FL 33767
- *Orere Source, The (Pastoral Abstracts),* P.O. Box 362, Harbert, MI 49115
- *Peace Research Abstracts Journal,* Peace Research Institute, 25 Dundana Avenue, Dundas, Ontario L9H 4ES, Canada

(continued)

- *Sage Race Relations Abstracts,* University of Manchester, Department of American Studies, Manchester M13 9PL, England
- *Sage Urban Studies Abstracts (SUSA),* Sage Publications, Inc., 2455 Teller Road, Newbury Park, CA 91320
- *Social Work Abstracts,* National Association of Social Workers, 750 First Street NW, 8th Floor, Washington, DC 20002
- *Sociological Abstracts (SA),* Sociological Abstracts, Inc., P.O. Box 22206, San Diego, CA 92192-0206
- *Theology Digest (also made available on CD-ROM),* St. Louis University, 3650 Lindell Boulevard, St. Louis, MO 63108
- *Violence and Abuse Abstracts: A Review of Current Literature on Interpersonal Violence (VAA),* Sage Publications, Inc., 2455 Teller Road, Newbury Park, CA 91320

SPECIAL BIBLIOGRAPHIC NOTES

*related to special journal issues (separates)
and indexing/abstracting*

☐ indexing/abstracting services in this list will also cover material in any "separate" that is co-published simultaneously with Haworth's special thematic journal issue or DocuSerial. Indexing/abstracting usually covers material at the article/chapter level.

☐ monographic co-editions are intended for either non-subscribers or libraries which intend to purchase a second copy for their circulating collections.

☐ monographic co-editions are reported to all jobbers/wholesalers/approval plans. The source journal is listed as the "series" to assist the prevention of duplicate purchasing in the same manner utilized for books-in-series.

☐ to facilitate user/access services all indexing/abstracting services are encouraged to utilize the co-indexing entry note indicated at the bottom of the first page of each article/chapter/contribution.

☐ this is intended to assist a library user of any reference tool (whether print, electronic, online, or CD-ROM) to locate the monographic version if the library has purchased this version but not a subscription to the source journal.

☐ individual articles/chapters in any Haworth publication are also available through the Haworth Document Delivery Service (HDDS).

ABOUT THE EDITORS

Roland G. Meinert, PhD, is President of the Missouri Association for Social Welfare in Jefferson City, Missouri. His previous positions include Director of the Schools of Social Work at Michigan State University and at the University of Missouri at Columbia. Dr. Meinert is the former co-editor of the journal *Social Development Issues* and has given numerous presentations on such topics as postmodernism, social development, social work administration, and educational technology.

John T. Pardeck, PhD, is Professor of Social Work in the School of Social Work at Southwest Missouri State University. He is a member of the Academy of Certified Social Workers (ACSW) and a Licensed Clinical Social Worker (LCSW) in the state of Missouri. Dr. Pardeck has published over 100 articles in academic and professional journals, as well as several books. His most recent books include *Computers in Human Services: An Overview for Clinical and Welfare Services* (1990); *The Computerization of Human Services Agencies: A Critical Appraisal* (1991); *Issues in Social Work: A Critical Analysis,* with Roland G. Meinert and William P. Sullivan (1994), and *Social Work Practice: An Ecological Approach* (1994).

John W. Murphy, PhD, is Professor of Sociology at the University of Miami. Dr. Murphy has taught classes on the topics of social problems, social theory, and the sociology of science, and he specializes in the areas of social theory and race and ethnicity. His articles have appeared in such journals as *Political Crossroads, Journal of Applied Gerontology,* and *Journal of Sociology and Social Welfare.* His most recent books include *Postmodernism, Unraveling Racism, Democratic Institutions, and Politics of Culture.*

Postmodernism, Religion and the Future of Social Work

CONTENTS

Introduction to Postmodernism, Religion and the Future of Social Work

Roland G. Meinert
John T. Pardeck
John W. Murphy

Social workers are beginning to use many of the concepts, perspectives and beliefs of postmodern philosophy even though clearcut definitions of it and specific guidelines for practice have not been developed. Their motivation in this regard is based on the recognition that contemporary social work practice has many epistemological and existential problems and they are turning to postmodernism to make sense out of a world that has become increasingly chaotic under conditions of modernity. In turning to a new set of beliefs they view reality not only in terms of what has gone before, defined by terms such as "post" industrial and "post" modern, but also in terms of a world view that is emerging along indeterminate and ambiguous lines. Because postmodernism is rapidly assuming a more prominent place in social work this special edition was designed to analytically explore several of the issues that are inherent to the perspective.

The first usage of the term was around 1870 by an English painter, John Watkins Chapman, who spoke of "postmodern paintings" that were, in his view, more modern than French impressionists. For the past century literature, art, and the humanities have been

[Haworth co-indexing entry note]: "Introduction to Postmodernism, Religion and the Future of Social Work." Meinert, Roland G., John T. Pardeck, and John W. Murphy. Co-published simultaneously in *Social Thought* (The Haworth Pastoral Press, an imprint of The Haworth Press, Inc.) Vol. 18, No. 3, 1998, pp. 1-4; and: *Postmodernism, Religion and the Future of Social Work* (ed: Roland G. Meinert, John T. Pardeck, and John W. Murphy) The Haworth Pastoral Press, an imprint of The Haworth Press, Inc., 1998, pp. 1-4. Single or multiple copies of this article are available for a fee from The Haworth Document Delivery Service [1-800-342-9678, 9:00 a.m. - 5:00 p.m. (EST). E-mail address: getinfo@haworth.com].

1

strongly influenced by postmodern perspectives. Most experts now believe that a society structured along postmodern lines began to take shape in the advanced capitalist countries shortly after World War II. However, prior to this time some social scientists theorized about the effect of moving beyond modernity and the radical breaks that were taking place with history and tradition. In order to understand the effect of postmodern thinking on social work in the contemporary world, it is helpful to follow the changes in thinking by sociologists following the modern period. In the first article in this special edition, John Murphy and John Pardeck describe the developments that have shaped postmodern thinking as they pertain to society in general and social work in particular. In their view, postmodern social work is not the wave of the future but has already arrived, and they describe the sociological developments upon which it is founded.

Since the debatable failure of the Great Society and the community mental health movement, many questions have arisen about the scientific model upon which the profession of social work was founded. Specifically under attack have been empirically based methodologies; the construct of objective reality; the belief in the neutrality of the practitioner; the social worker as expert knower; and others. In their article Weick and Saleebey argue that the longstanding dependence of social work on a logical positivist epistemology is inappropriate for the malleable world in which clients live and the associated problems they face. In their view, the emerging strengths perspective in social work fits well the conceptual parameters of postmodernism. It moves beyond the sterile elements of logical positivism and focuses on the talents and abilities of clients within the traditional person in the environment configuration. In their view, postmodern social work within the strengths perspective will be more relevant and humane.

The bulk of social work literature about postmodernism is of a supportive nature in that it presents the relevance of the perspective to practice situations. In some instances this literature is exploratory in nature and urges practitioners to adopt it as an organizing modality. None of the literature about postmodernism and social work has specifically attempted to identify the potential negative effects of the movement. The article by Meinert deals with some of the negative and unintended consequences of the postmodern influence in social work. Several postmodern tenets are reviewed and they are related to outcomes that could be damaging to the profession. Meinert advises caution in uncritically adopting postmodernism as a foundation for both social work practice and education.

On the face of it, postmodernism would seem to be entirely antithetical to the provision of social services and social work practice based in religious auspiced agencies. Institutional religion emphasizes absolute or fundamental principles about life whereas postmodernism is founded on indeterminate and relativistic beliefs. Hutchison examines this issue from several perspectives. In logical progression he distinguishes spirituality from institutionalized religion and then shows the compatibility of spirituality with postmodernism. Having established these connections he presents data documenting the extensive allocation of resources by religiously auspiced social services which do not depend on creedal affiliations by client populations.

Postmodern thinking and its relevance to social services and social problems appeared on the European continent before it arrived in the United States. There are lessons to be learned from the experience in Britain with social services with a postmodern influence. Parton describes the perspectives associated with postmodernity, postmodernization and post-Fordism in relation to British social services. He concludes that these developments do signify the nature of current times but lack explanatory power in explaining them. In his view, the changes taking place in contemporary society are better characterized in terms of advanced liberalism or extended liberal modernity rather than postmodernism per se. In his view, postmodern tenets are simply a mirror to a society that is increasingly fragmented and segregated. He questions whether postmodernism offers definitive answers as to how conditions can be improved and how the quality of improvements might be judged.

There is great appeal on the part of the postmodern perspective in regard to the pervasive social problems that exist in the United States. In some respects it offers a new and different way of understanding social problems and of structuring social work practice. However, like earlier models for explanation and application such as psychoanalysis, role theory, and systems theory, it should not be adopted in an uncritical fashion by practitioners. The intent of this special edition about postmodernism and social work was designed to explore several of the issues about which final answers have not appeared. In a postmodern world and a postmodern profession characterized by ongoing change, indeterminacy and relativism it is absolutely necessary to continue an ongoing dialogue about challenging perspectives for day-to-day practice.

Renewing Social Work Practice Through a Postmodern Perspective

John W. Murphy
John T. Pardeck

SUMMARY. Postmodernism is one of the most recent significant developments within the social sciences. This paper reviews the movement toward a postmodern perspective beginning in the late 19th century in the field of sociology. The evolution toward a postmodern perspective in the social sciences has important implications for the profession of social work. The authors suggest that the postmodern perspective has the potential to renew the profession of social work. *[Article copies available for a fee from The Haworth Document Delivery Service: 1-800-342-9678. E-mail address: getinfo@haworth.com]*

Postmodernism is probably one of the most significant intellectual developments in recent years (Ritzer, 1992). Variations of the postmodern movement are emerging in all fields of the social sciences including social work. One of the clear strengths of postmodernism is the emphasis that it places on diversity of ideas, a perspective highly compatible with the profession of social work.

A postmodern point of view rejects objectivism and absolutionism and stresses pluralism, relativism, and flexibility (Laird, 1993).

John W. Murphy, PhD, Department of Sociology, Miami University, Coral Gables, FL 33124.

John T. Pardeck, PhD, ACSW, School of Social Work, Southwest Missouri State University, Springfield, MO 65804.

[Haworth co-indexing entry note]: "Renewing Social Work Practice Through a Postmodern Perspective." Murphy, John W., and John T. Pardeck. Co-published simultaneously in *Social Thought* (The Haworth Pastoral Press, an imprint of The Haworth Press, Inc.) Vol. 18, No. 3, 1998, pp. 5-19; and: *Postmodernism, Religion and the Future of Social Work* (ed: Roland G. Meinert, John T. Pardeck, and John W. Murphy) The Haworth Pastoral Press, an imprint of The Haworth Press, Inc., 1998, pp. 5-19. Single or multiple copies of this article are available for a fee from The Haworth Document Delivery Service [1-800-342-9678, 9:00 a.m. - 5:00 p.m. (EST). E-mail address: getinfo@haworth.com].

5

The postmodern perspective challenges old theories, in particular those grounded in the modern world, and calls for new paradigms. The movement toward a postmodern perspective in the social sciences has its roots in 19th century sociology. The purpose of this paper is to trace this historical development and to discuss the implications of the postmodern movement on the profession of social work.

TRADITIONAL SOCIOLOGY AND SOCIAL ORDER

Positivism emerged within the field of sociology in the late 19th century. A number of early social theorists, specifically Comte and Durkheim, viewed the social changes occurring in the late 19th century as a threat to the social and moral order of France (Aron, 1968). Positivism was seen as a scientific theory that would offer strategies for effectively dealing with the perceived breakdown of society.

Comte and Durkheim argued that the spiritual and moral crises facing France could be resolved through positivism (Aron, 1968). They felt that positivism would provide the scientific based knowledge needed to replace social theories and philosophies largely built on speculation. The positivist approach emphasized that knowledge should be based on facts derived from science. Positivism provided a new epistemology that would offer social order to societies on the verge of social chaos.

Much of the change occurring in France in the late 19th century was due to industrialization. Industrialization brought growth and diversity, as well as a middle class that scoffed at tradition. Along with an increase in new wealth among the middle class, a proletarian class was also burgeoning. To Comte and Durkheim, these class divisions signaled the onset of *anomie*. Traditional values were disappearing that were thought to be essential to maintaining social order within civilization.

A *laissez-faire* philosophy often associated with Adam Smith also began to take root (Aron, 1968). The best society was viewed by some as one based on marketplace principles; thus the pursuit of individual economic gain was viewed as positive. However, Comte and Durkheim felt the laissez-faire philosophy had great limitations. They concluded that a laissez-faire approach to organizing society created individuals who were so absorbed in their own self-interests that traditional norms would gradually break down. No society, reasoned Comte and Durkheim, could survive without a universal set of values, or a melange of competing claims would ultimately destroy social order (Aron, 1968). Positivism was viewed as a scientific approach that would prevent such chaos.

Comte and Durkheim, both social realists, contended that knowledge and order are autonomous, and thus these factors did not depend on individuals for their creation. This position is clearly dualistic, in that facts and norms are assumed to be categorically removed from the human experience.

Due to their faith in science, Comte and Durkheim argued that through the use of logic and experimentation a uniform knowledge base could be generated to guide social development. Both theorists stressed that knowledge could be generated through science. Because experimentation was believed to be value-free, objective knowledge would be produced through science. Scientific facts, as described by Durkheim, are external and independent of the social world. Facts exist external to the human mind, are context-independent, and can be discovered through science. In this sense, Durkheim (1976, p. 58) argued that facts should be treated as "things," because they are "not naturally controlled by the intellect and cannot be adequately grasped by a simple process of mental activity."

In the positive stage of historical development, scientific facts were allotted a seigniorial status. This position is illustrated neatly in Durkheim's (1983) lectures on pragmatism, which he delivered at the Sorbonne during the 1913-14 academic year. He argued that pragmatism was problematic because this philosophy suggests truth is synonymous with individual proclivities. As might be suspected, he argued that such an approach to the discovery of truth could only culminate in chaos. Durkheim maintained that truth had to be impersonal and extra-individual. Understood this way, truth exists outside the social world and could be discovered through positivism.

Comte and Durkheim viewed society as similar to a living organism analogous to the human body. Similar to the organs of the human body, social institutions work in harmony with one another and perform functions that are vital to the survival of the whole organism. Most important, each component is subordinate to the whole and guided by the *telos* that is assumed to be directing the operation of the body. Again consistent with realism, society is given primacy over the individual. "What is social," notes Durkheim (1983, p. 68), "always possesses a higher dignity than what is individual." In essence, the individual's purpose is derived from the needs of the society.

European sociological theory heavily influenced the development of sociology in the United States. During what is called the period of Early American sociology (1881-1930), two themes were prominent. The first was an interest in making sociology a positive science. Therefore, several methodological disputes were given attention. And second, organicism was revived in the form of a unique evolutionary theory that was underpinned by the notion that society could be improved through social engineering based on scientific principles.

Early American sociology lacked sophistication and had little impact on modern day sociological theory. A developed sociological theory of society emerged in the 1950s in the writings of Parsons (1951). Parsons' systems theory of society was comprehensive, grounded in science, and supposedly offered an objective approach to the study of society. Parsons' work, specifically, popularized the metaphor of social systems. This metaphor has had a tremendous influence on modern social work systems theory. Similar to Comte and Durkheim, Parsons had a negative view of human behavior. Parsons suggested that without some kind of external constraint, social chaos would result.

Parsons suggested that persons could not be trusted to regulate themselves, because of their improvident character. Therefore, Parsons (1951) concluded that order would prevail only if individuals were structurally linked together. Parsons (1951, p. 36) envisioned society as a system of specific roles, which are in a state of "double contingency." These roles, in other words, are linked through reciprocal obligations and sanctions. As opposed to volition and agreement, roles are united because of structural and functional necessity. The linkage between roles is thus guaranteed despite human involvement with the larger social system.

Postmodernism suggests that social cooperation can be achieved in a variety of ways. For example, persons can reach a consensus through dialogue. This rendition of order, however, is predicated on the vision that individuals are not atoms who are mostly self-consumed. But at least until the mid-1960s, most sociologists were not optimistic about this prospect. Consequently, Dennis Wrong (1961) concluded that mainstream sociologists cling to an oversocialized concept of man, whereby order is thought to be impossible without outside influences. Some type of autonomous apparatus, unadulterated by human bias, is required to secure order.

Social Realism

There is little doubt that order can be reinforced by the realism adhered to by conventional sociologists. But, as suggested by Wrong (1961), there is a significant downside to this theoretical approach. Dehumanization can become commonplace, once realism is invoked to justify the maintenance of order. As C. Wright Mills (1951) described in his now classic critique of Parsons, reality is elevated to such importance that the human element is either overlooked or imagined to pose a threat to the social order. The result is the "hypostatization of society"(O'Dea, 1970, p. 234). This kind of abstract theorizing prompted Homans (1964) to conclude that "men should be brought back into" the scope of sociology.

The social realism indicative of much of modern day sociological theory, such as systems theory, has heavily influenced the applied professions such as social work. These theories have the potential to dehumanize. The following examples illustrate the potential dehumanizing effects of modern sociological theory, particularly systems theory. In each example, persons are stripped of the ability to shape reality; at best, they only respond to social conditions.

1. For the most part, in modern day sociological theory, persons are portrayed as beings shaped largely by their social environment, obviously a view also well-grounded in social work thought. Individuals are believed to be prompted into action by either stimuli, system imperatives, or the demands issued by roles. That persons might have a real self, as opposed to a social identity, is not an awareness promoted by traditional realists. In point of fact, emphasizing role making, and not

simply role taking, was initiated by critics of functionalism (Turner, 1962).

2. Research is associated with empiricism. This outcome is logical, given the stress that has been placed on objectivity. Nonetheless, the variables that are believed to affect behavior, including personal traits, have been conceptualized as empirical indicators. C. Wright Mills (1951) referred to this research strategy as "abstract empiricism." Distorted by this practice, however, are factors that cannot be translated readily into empirical indices, such as linguistic acts, symbols, and other modes of interpretation.

3. Explanations for behavior tend to become very abstract. For example, in the field of social work, this is one of the core criticisms practitioners have of systems theory. In fact, sociologism is the term that has been used to describe the focus placed on the social system (Tiryakian, 1963). What is meant by this idea is that the system is identified as causing behavior. Rather than human agents, for example, social change is purported to result in role strain (Parsons, 1951). The key explanatory factor is the system's response to innovation, as opposed to the actual proposals or mandates that are issued by individuals or groups. In this case, change is not humanly inspired but mechanistic.

4. The thrust of this realistic analysis has been insuring compliance with the social system. Restoring reason or health, for example, has meant rehabilitating people to perform their social roles. Furthermore, deviance and other instances of maladjustment have been defined as violations of systemic norms. As demonstrated most recently by Michel Foucault (1989), rationality and logic are presumed to be properties of the social system–the disciplinary apparatus–and not human actors. What persons understand to be rational action is treated as incidental.

In the end, roles are more important than those who fulfill these interlocking sets of expectations. Yet during the mid- to late-1960s this tendency began to be challenged. What might be called an interpretive turn was inaugurated, which attempted to resurrect the human element that was obscured by the social system. The aim was to illustrate that the system is not autonomous, but a human creation.

The Interpretive Turn

Symbolic interactionism grew out of the work of G. H. Mead (Ritzer, 1992). Mead, like other pragmatists, was rebelling against empiricism. Reducing the world to the sum of sense impressions created serious problems for understanding social life. As described by William James, existence as suggested by empiricists consists of little more than booming, buzzing confusion (Blumer, 1969). In other words, thoughts and actions are simply comprised of concatenated sensory data.

Contrary to this scenario, Mead argued that at the core of behavior is "the Act." Rather than passively absorbing input, persons are actively involved in defining, selecting, and manipulating objects. Individuals engage the world and give it meaning, and accordingly continue to behave in terms of the resulting body of information. "Meanings are social products . . . creations that are formed in and through the defining activities of people as they interact"(Blumer, 1969, p. 5). Hence persons do not inhabit a world of empirical objects, but instead act on the basis of meanings that are socially constituted. To borrow a term from existentialism, reality is a product of the human experience.

According to Mead's key student, Herbert Blumer, this theoretical demarche meant that the traditional renditions of society had to be rethought. Blumer (1969) insisted that mechanistic, organismic, and systems analogies are too abstract and misrepresent social life. Consistent with Mead's anti-dualistic stance, Blumer argued that order had to emerge from human action. For nothing, even structural imperatives, is immune to the mental process whereby meanings are created. Therefore, Blumer (1969) concluded that order is revealed through recurrent patterns of joint action. He goes on to suggest that social reality represents interaction between *people* and not between roles. Through what Mead calls a conversation of gestures, persons recognize each other's interpretation of events and try not to transgress these intended meanings (Ritzer, 1992).

Particularly in the 1960s, many sociologists found symbolic interactionism to be liberating. No longer did persons have to be portrayed as beings ensnared within a larger social system. Instead, persons were suddenly free to propose alternative realities. But some critics thought that symbolic interactionism did not go far enough. A residue of dualism remained, as witnessed in Mead's distinction between symbolic and non-symbolic objects, that legitimized the autonomy of the social system. But during a period when such realism was held in contempt, the stage was set for the acceptance of any theory that appeared less dualistic than symbolic interactionism.

With the publication of Peter Berger and Thomas Luckmann's *Social Construction of Reality* (1966), American social scientists were introduced to phenomenology. These authors borrowed heavily from Alfred Schutz and, in turn, began to call the social world the *Lebenswelt*, or "life-world." Giving credence to the phenomenological notion of intentionality, Berger and Luckmann's views were seen as more radical than symbolic interactionists'. That is, reality could not be separated from conscious activity.

Husserl's (1975, p. 23) simple phrase "consciousness is always conscious of something," is the essence of intentionality, and has had a significant impact on sociology. Any remnant of dualism left behind by symbolic interactionism was eradicated. From now on, everything that is known had to be understood as thoroughly inundated by consciousness. Facts, accordingly, were understood to be socially mediated. Truth, moreover, was defined in terms of coherence, continuity, or consistency. And rather than a stream of empirical facts and events, the social *Lebenswelt* was identified to consist of a network of meanings that are existential in origin. Reality has a fleshy character, according to Merleau-Ponty (1968), because human action and whatever is known are inextricably linked.

The vital shortcoming of phenomenology, claimed its opponents, is that this philosophy is merely a rendition of idealism, and therefore ignores the material conditions of existence. In modern parlance, issues of class, race, and gender were barely mentioned (Coser, 1975). To correct this omission, a variation of Marxism was introduced. However, those that dealt with the structural side of the capitalist economy were dismissed as dualistic, crudely materialistic, and insensitive to the repressive culture of capitalism. On the other hand, theories proposed to address the issue of *Praxis*, and therefore undermine dualism and temper materialism, were labeled revisionistic and disqualified as ineffectual.

Out of this condition emerged a philosophy that is strangely Marxist and overtly linguistic. The dangerous nature of this outlook became immediately apparent, as witnessed by the criticisms of postmodernism in the mainstream press. Postmodernism, in one form or another, is viewed by many as a threat to culture, morality and order. D'Sousa's (1991) characterization of the postmodernist Stanley Fish, as an agent provocateur, exemplifies the treatment of this philosophy.

Postmodernists such as Roland Barthes, Jacques Derrida, Stanley Fish, Jacques Lacan, and Jean-Francois Lyotard argue that nothing transcends the influence of language. Barthes (1985, p. 271) concludes that everything is language, and nothing escapes language, that is, all of society is permeated by language. Postmodernism rejects dualism, and thus suggests reality is discovered within the context of speech. "Objectivity," remarks Barthes (1985, p. 27), "is only one image-repertoire among others. Reality is a linguistic habit."

According to postmodernists, intentionality is an activity that is too ethereal to depict the formation of reality. Substituted in place of this idea is language. Language is both tangible and flexible, and thus social reality is described as layers of interpretation. In this sense, the trend initiated by symbolic interactionism was brought to fruition by postmodernism. At the foundation of norms, customs, and laws is symbolism that cannot escape the dynamics and openness of language use.

LANGUAGE, KNOWLEDGE, AND ORDER

Lyotard's *Postmodern Condition* (1984) has become tantamount to the manifesto of the postmodern movement. Issues related to knowledge and order are addressed in this book in a much more comprehensive way than in other postmodern tracts. What he offers in this book serves as an excellent introduction to important postmodern themes.

Lyotard (1984, p. XXIV) defines postmodernism as "incredulity toward metanarratives." These Grand Narratives are exemplified by Durkheim's (1976) notion of reality *"sui generis."* Reality is held together by these stories because they transcend the exigencies of daily life. But postmodernists contend that these abstractions are no longer available to underpin order. The rationale for this loss is simple: the dualism that substantiates the schism between the mundane and sublime is passé. There is no ultimate reality.

Dualism is defunct because of the theory of language adhered to by postmodernists. Lyotard (1984) resorts to the work of Ludwig Wittgenstein to detail the relationship between language and reality. Contrary to the standard theory of language, which has its origins in Mead, Wittgenstein (1953) asserts that all knowledge is mediated by interpretation. Rather than mimicking reality, language shapes whatever is known. Language has a pragmatic thrust that is indispensable in securing the identity of any phenomenon. As suggested by Barthes (1985), there is nothing to explore outside of language. Language is not transparent and thus leads to an unadulterated reality. In this regard, Fish (1989, p. 314) concludes that "questions of fact, truth, correctness, validity, and clarity can neither be posed nor answered in reference to some extra contextual, historical, non-situated reality." These issues are settled only from within the folds of language.

Does this conclusion signal the end of objective knowledge, as the critics of postmodernism claim? Lyotard says no. Nonetheless, the usual version of facts as context-independent, empirical entities must be revised. What transforms empirical markers into something meaningful are the assumptions made about reality that are linguistically instituted. "What anyone sees," claims Fish (1989, p. 34), "is not independent of his verbal and mental categories but is in fact a product of them." All so-called empirical indices, therefore, are already interpreted before they are supposedly encountered and described.

But without the presence of an unbiased spectator, do facts dissolve into ambiguity? Since the early 1900s the answer to this query has been no. With the proper qualifications, knowledge can be identified and treated as factual. Following the specification, dissemination, and acceptance of certain assumptions, accessibility to data can be provided. And once this context is established, facts can be said to exist. In this sense, Barthes (1987, p. 39) writes that even "evident truths are only choices."

Rather than being a spectacle, facts are embedded within language. Instead of universal facts, facts are historical and regional. Lyotard (1984), for example, relies on the work of Rene Thorn to substantiate this conclusion. Thorn, the founder of Catastrophe Theory, argues that reality is not smooth and continuous (Lyotard, 1984). Contrary to this picture, reality consists of a patchwork with disjunctures between the pieces. And movement from one path to another may precipitate a crisis, or catastrophe, because different rules about reality may be operative in these locations.

"All that exist," claims Lyotard (1984, p. 54), "are islands of determinism." Rules certainly exist, but only in particular locales. Lyotard's point of mentioning this theory is to suggest that knowledge is stable, and even predictable within specific situations, but is not necessarily universal. Universality is a property, within catastrophe theory, that must be socially constituted. As opposed to a grand narrative, each locale represents a petite narrative of a story that has regional legitimacy. The key to understanding is comprehending the "language game" that is operative in each case.

Given the ubiquity of language, as might be suspected, Lyotard (1984) proposes that society is not a totality. The reason why these models are invalid is that language is not easily idealized; interpretation is not easily universalized. Instead, society consists of what Lyotard (1984, p. 59) describes as "flexible networks of language games."

The social bond, accordingly, is also linguistic. This is the outcome that symbolic interactionists wanted to foster, yet they seemed to have vacillated on this issue. Contrary to what Blumer intended, role making and role taking are often differentiated, thereby suggesting that roles exist prior to being made. Lyotard (1984) is adamant to reflect this style of dualism, which he believes reifies society. He concludes that a fictional account of order such as this is not required to hold society together. Rather than abstract, the social bond is a fabric formed by the intersection of at least two (and in reality an indeterminate number) of language games, obeying different rules. At the nexus of speech acts, simply put, is where order is engendered and maintained.

According to Lyotard (1984), persons have the ability to become reflexive and review critically their own linguistic moves and gambits made by others. The result of this activity is that order is fundamentally intersubjective, or based on interlocutors coordinating their linguistic moves. Order, therefore, can be stable, but further modification of any pattern is always possible. As Lyotard (1984, p. 64) writes, any consensus *"must be local, in other words, agreed on by its present players and subject to eventual cancellation."* Order is not sabotaged, as postmodernism's critics report, but merely versions that rest on realist pretensions.

TOWARD A RENEWED SOCIAL WORK PRACTICE

Social work practice can be enhanced through the postmodern perspective. Postmodernism celebrates diversity and suggests that reality is largely shaped by each individual. What this means is there is no ultimate "objective reality," reality is situational and community based. For example, what it means to be poor, homeless, an old person, or a person with a disability is largely defined by persons experiencing each of these personal situations; reality for each of these situations is defined by the person and shaped by other social systems such as a family, group, or organization (Fisher, 1991). Practitioners must be sensitive to these definitions in order to conduct appropriate assessments and interventions.

The disabilities civil rights movement is an excellent example for illustrating the importance of enhancing practice and policy through the postmodern perspective. Clearly, science has been used for decades as the medium for defining the meaning of disability. The scientific view of disability, which has greatly influenced the larger society's perception of this phenomenon, suggests that a disability is found within the person (Pardeck, 1994). The disabilities civil rights movement has challenged this notion and argues that the meaning of a disability is found outside the self and is simply a social construction of society. This shift has resulted in empowerment of persons with disabilities and calls for a dramatic shift in how one conducts social work practice when dealing with this new minority group.

What is powerful about a postmodern approach to practice is that it demystifies traditional theories and limits their authority in defining social reality. As suggested by the historical development of postmodernism, accepted social scientific theories are often an extension of a dominant group's self-interests and its ideologies. The social realities experienced by oppressed groups are typically greatly different from those of the dominant group. A postmodern view suggests that the perceptions of social reality as defined by all groups are equally relevant for understanding the social world.

A postmodern view concludes there is not an ultimate authoritative source of knowledge. For example, empirically based research is treated with the same respect as other sources of knowledge. A post-modern worldview suggests that knowledge is constructed through language and that facts are embedded within language. Social work practitioners must be sensitive to these notions when conducting assessments and when delivering services. In other words, social intervention must be truly "community based." The following summarizes the core ideas critical to a postmodern perspective to social work.

1. Reality must be treated as socially constructed through language use. Norms, customs, and rituals, for example, are locally designated. Perelman's (1979) distinction between reasonable and rational behavior is instructive at this juncture. His point is that no behavior is ultimately rational, but rather acts make sense in terms of their social context. Professional judgements about normalcy or illness, accordingly, should reflect these various boundaries.

2. The methods used to gather information about clients, the knowledge base for clinical decision making, should be attuned to the different language games that are operative in society. Therefore, research instruments should be viewed as the means for engaging persons, such as clients, in dialogue. But this is not the image of research that is usually presented. Instead, emphasis is typically placed on value freedom and maintaining a significant amount of distance from those who are studied. This *modus operandi* is thought to guarantee objectivity. Most important in view of postmodernism, however, should be contextual sensitivity.

3. The interventions that are chosen should reflect, in Fish's words (1980, p. 171), the "interpretive community" in question. What constitutes an appropriate intervention, successful

treatment, or correct policy, for example, should be viewed as a local determination. The norms of the *Lebenswelt* should be employed to guide rehabilitation. As Ludwig Binswanger points out, a person's mode of being-in-the world should dictate the need and course of treatment (Binswanger, 1963). Social treatment should lead, in other words, and should not be prescribed by the requirements of an abstract social system.

4. The ethical principle that should guide intervention is to protect the integrity of a client's world-view. This position is different from that advanced by Durkheim or Parsons, for example, who maintain that the aim of intervention should be to restore harmony to the social system. As a result, the individual or community is sacrificed to some greater whole. But the abstract universal that sustains this ethic is defunct as a result of postmodernism. The only exemplar that is available to ground an ethic is a patchwork of differences. Suggested by this framework is that the maintenance of these differences, as opposed to assimilation to an absolute ideal, should be the aim of intervention.

Finally, the general thrust of postmodernism has been to view social life as replete with possibilities. Without a doubt, the linguistic social bond proposed by postmodernists is more amenable to alteration and expansion than the standard structural version. Stanley Fish (1989) is careful to indicate, nonetheless, that this rendition of order does not immobilize persons and foster anarchy, due to an alleged absence of norms.

Norms are local, but can be expanded. The point is that the choice is no longer between postmodernism and universal bases of order. Through intersubjective activity, sometimes known as the realm of the "intertextual," order can be engendered (Pardeck, Murphy, and Chung, 1994). The message for social work practitioners is that social intervention is also an intersubjective endeavor. For example, social treatment is a cooperative (relational) venture that is designed to protect personal or collective differences, thereby enlarging the social mosaic. This approach to intervention is anarchistic only to those who labor to repair an ailing social system. But to postmodernists, this imagery is too abstract and incapable of dealing with the diversity that has come to characterize American life.

REFERENCES

Aron, R. (1968). *Main currents in sociological thought I.* Garden City, NY: Doubleday.

Barthes, R. (1987). *Criticism and truth.* Minneapolis: University of Minnesota Press.

Barthes, Roland (1985). *The grain of the voice.* NY: Hill and Wang.

Berger, P. L. & Luckmann, T. (1966). *The social construction of reality.* Garden City, NY: Doubleday.

Binswanger, L. (1963). *Being-in-the-world.* New York: Basic Books.

Blumer, H. (1969). *Symbolic interactionism: Perspective and method.* Englewood Cliffs, NJ: Prentice Hall.

Coser, L. (1975). Presidential address: Two methods in search of a substance. *American Sociological Review* 40, 691-700.

D'Sousa, D. (1991). *Illiberal education.* New York: The Free Press.

Derrida, J. (1976). *Of grammatology.* Baltimore: Johns Hopkins University Press.

Durkheim, E. (1976). *Selected writings.* Cambridge, MA: Cambridge University Press,

Durkheim, E. (1983). *Pragmatism and sociology.* Cambridge, MA: Cambridge University Press.

Fish, S. (1980). *Is there a text in this class?* Cambridge, MA: Harvard University Press.

Fish, S. (1989). *Doing what comes naturally.* Durham, NC: Duke University Press.

Fisher, D. D. V. (1991). *An introduction to constructivism for social workers.* New York: Praeger.

Foucault, M. (1973). *Madness and civilization.* New York: Vintage.

Homans, G. C. (1964). Bringing men back in. *American Sociological Review*, 29, pp. 809-815.

Husserl, E. (1975). *Paris lectures.* The Hague: Nijhoff.

Laird, J. (1993). Introduction. *Journal of Teaching in Social Work*, 8, 1-10.

Lyotard, J. (1984). *The postmodern condition: A report on knowledge.* Minneapolis: University of Minnesota Press.

Mills, C. W. (1959). *The sociological imagination.* London: Oxford University Press.

O'Dea, T. F. (1970). *Sociology and the study of religion.* New York: Basic Books.

Pardeck, J.T. (1994). What you need to know about the Americans with disabilities act. *Coping*, July/August, 16-17.

Pardeck, J.T., Murphy, J.W. and Chung, W.S. (1994). Social Work and Postmodernism, *Social Work and Social Science Review*, 5 (2), pp. 113-123.

Parsons, T. (1951). *The social system.* Glencoe, IL: The Free Press.

Perelman, C. (1979). *The new rhetoric and the humanities.* Dordrecht: D. Reidel.

Ritzer, G. (1992). *Contemporary sociological theory* (3rd ed.). New York: McGraw-Hill.

Turner, R. (1962). Role taking: Process versus conformity. In A. M. Rose (Ed.), *Human behavior and social process.* Boston: Houghton Mifflin.

Wittgenstein, W. (1953). *Philosophical investigations.* New York: Blackwell.

Wrong, D. (1961). The oversocialized conception of man in modern society, *American Sociological Review*, 26, 183-193.

Postmodern Perspectives for Social Work

Ann Weick
Dennis Saleebey

SUMMARY. This article concludes that the long-standing dependence of social work on positivism is no longer relevant for the profession. The authors argue that the strengths perspective supports a postmodern approach to practice and moves the profession beyond logical positivism. A postmodern approach to social work supports the strengths perspective and will enhance the person-in-the-environment approach to practice. *[Article copies available for a fee from The Haworth Document Delivery Service: 1-800-342-9678. E-mail address: getinfo @haworth.com]*

Social work has had a difficult time finding an intellectual home for its moral commitments. Its earliest impulses were fed by religious convictions about the nature of human struggles and the excesses of industrial society. At the center of these doctrines were beliefs about the capacity of human beings for personal transformation and opportunities in the social environment for supporting human needs. However, the goal of becoming a credible profession led social work along a path that overshadowed the power of these insights. Thus began the quest for a conceptual or theoretical frame-

Ann Weick, PhD, and Dennis Saleebey, DSW, are affiliated with the University of Kansas, School of Social Welfare, Lawrence, KS 66045.

This paper is based on a presentation for the Richard Lodge Memorial Lecture, October 1995, Adelphi University School of Social Work.

[Haworth co-indexing entry note]: "Postmodern Perspectives for Social Work." Weick, Ann, and Dennis Saleebey. Co-published simultaneously in *Social Thought* (The Haworth Pastoral Press, an imprint of The Haworth Press, Inc.) Vol. 18, No. 3, 1998, pp. 21-40; and: *Postmodernism, Religion and the Future of Social Work* (ed: Roland G. Meinert, John T. Pardeck, and John W. Murphy) The Haworth Pastoral Press, an imprint of The Haworth Press, Inc., 1998, pp. 21-40. Single or multiple copies of this article are available for a fee from The Haworth Document Delivery Service [1-800-342-9678, 9:00 a.m. - 5:00 p.m. (EST). E-mail address: getinfo@haworth.com].

21

work that would assure that social work would become a recognized profession and be allowed to contribute its special skills and orientation to society.

Retaining the character of social work as a moral and civic enterprise has produced a creative tension throughout this development. The impulse to professionalize practice drove social work to borrow theories whole cloth from other disciplines, resulting in the promulgation of approaches that did not explicitly reflect social work values. At the same time, the development of theory based on the client's lifeworld has received little attention or approbation. The painful division between academic social work and social work practice is merely an external sign of the profession's persistent inability to develop conceptions of its practice which successfully articulate the robust practice knowledge and wisdom lying in the marrow of our profession.

During the last 15 years, there has been a significant development of perspectives both within and outside the field which challenge some of the current conceptions and approaches to social work practice. They share a common ground of assumptions, values and methods which bring into clearer focus the professional commitments of social work and thus hold promise for healing the rift between what we know, what we do, and why we do it.

The early moral and social orientations of the profession run deep in memory but they have become part of an increasingly silent language as the weight of the scientific world view suppressed these appreciations. The translation of scientific assumptions and methods from the natural world to the physical world, to the social world and, ultimately, to the human/interpersonal world was a feat of astonishing hubris, with long-lived consequences (Weick, 1987, 1991; Rosaldo, 1989). To imagine that the human world was amenable to the application of principles and formulae derived from the study of rocks and trees presented significant challenges to human understanding and social action. Yet an empirically-based methodology, and positivist philosophy with its attendant assumptions of objective reality, observer neutrality, and technical rationality (Schon, 1983) has, for the past 50 years, posed as the preeminent paradigm of knowledge for the social sciences and the professions. The outgrowth of this tilt toward empiricism has been the notable absence of concern for philosophical and theoretical issues and a willingness to allow most practice issues and questions to be decided by method (Saleebey, 1993, p. 6).

Academic social work has been zealous in its promotion of the scientific method as the basis for practice. The pleas for a more rationalized and scientific practice came as early as Mary Richmond (1917) and Bertha Reynolds (1942). However, their interest in a less moralistic, more systematic approach seems sweetly naive in the face of the more strenuous arguments carried forward as the 20th century has unfolded (Fischer, 1981; Hudson, 1982; Grinnell et al., 1995). The recent report of the Task Force on Social Work Research (1991) is only the most current example of a significant effort by academicians to prevail upon the profession to conform to more rigorous methodological standards in research and to more closely align practice with the technologies and orientation of science.

While the effort to scientize and rationalize practice has moved steadily forward, there has been a countervailing movement most easily captured in the lament about the division between research and practice. In spite of a well-organized effort to encourage practitioners to become more scientific, most practitioners have purposively or hesitantly gone in search of clinical approaches which promise to make the mysteries of the helping process more accessible. For some, the wisdom gleaned from classroom and field experience has created a base sufficient for versatile and well-grounded practice. Others draw on more eclectic and plentiful sources: solution-focused family therapy, the recovery movement and addictions treatment, pop psychology, self-help groups, to name a few. These approaches seem to offer the imagery, power and richness of human experience so frequently lacking in more prosaic strategies advertised in many social work texts. Because these other approaches tend to engage practitioners in a more visceral way, their basic assumptions often go unexamined. The fact that they may place the practitioners in the role of expert, that they may incorporate an elaborate vocabulary of pathology or that they may require people to pursue a plan not of their own making may slip by unnoticed. In both cases, social workers often practice in a shadow world, without the full approval of their academic colleagues, their professional colleagues or the general public. Social workers' multiple talents add to the well-being of their clients, the organizations in which they work and to the community but sometimes these are bathed in an apology for not being able to be clearer about what social workers really do.

If it is true that social work's vision is illuminated by philosophical and conceptual connections that cannot be properly articulated and realized within current technologically oriented perspectives, then it is important to search for other intellectual affiliations. Fortunately, there have been developments that are available to help design a different paradigm for social work. The strengths perspective within social work and the viewpoint illuminated by social constructivism, holistic health, resilience and the mind-body relationship provide an avenue for extending the philosophical claims of the profession in ways that more powerfully capture the essential commitments underlying good social work practice. Their common assumptions reflect a strategy for consciously digging from the earthy roots of social work wisdom a ground of understanding that evokes an essential realignment with our moral and civil covenants.

THE POSTMODERN WORLD

In the past fifty years, the pillars of a dominant world view have begun to develop visible cracks. The scientific paradigm, which has held sway for over 400 years, has extended our capacity to explore, monitor and master some elements of the social and natural worlds. As a major epistemology, it has ground a lens through which many see the world. Inevitably and regrettably, that lens cannot bring light to another world, for it was cut to reflect on that which is palpable and measurable.

The most salient characteristic of both the medieval and modern world views has been their foundationalism. Both systems of thought posited a knowable reality which could serve as a foundation or bedrock for the pursuit of truth. In the medieval view, reason enlightened by faith was the path of God-ordained truth. In the scientific world view, reason aided by empirically based, logically wrought experiments has been the route to knowledge. Both rest on the assumption that the worlds of nature, society and human behavior can be studied in ways which correspond to a reality independent from and unaffected by human processes and consciousness. The consequences of this assumption have been profound. Certain colors on the behavioral spectrum have been highlighted, others muted. Modern approaches to inquiry reify the skills of logic, rationality, analysis, technological invention, mathematical formulations and dispassionate observation. Technique and method, they assume, will be the ultimate arbiters of knowledge and practice. They dismiss as irrelevant or inferior routes to knowledge and understanding that are recursive, process oriented, indeterminate, and value based. Intuition, philosophy, dialogical exploration, dialectical exposition, empathic grasp, story, and artistry are regarded as not up to the task of discovering the truth of the matter. Modern approaches assign higher truth value to scientific research carried out according to strict methodological conditions than to methods of inquiry which seek to describe and reflect people's lived experience. They partialize the human condition into manageable segments for study, rather than explore patterned and unpatterned complexity.

In pursuing its methodological strategies, the scientific world view made the eighteenth century principles of faith in reason and human progress seem immanent and possible (Randall, 1976, p. 383). In all spheres of life, the positive impact of scientific developments has been the centerpiece of the modern age and has contributed to improvements in the human condition and in the human capacity to explore ever larger and smaller aspects of the world. However, the reach of science is now under serious criticism from virtually all segments of society (Schon, 1983; Tyson, 1995; Goldstein, 1986; Gergen, 1991). The events of World War II marked a shift in consciousness, where a guileless faith in the unmitigated benefits of technology and science was challenged by the appalling reality of atomic warfare and the scientifically glossed attempt to create a master race through systematic genocide (Rifkin, 1985; Berman, 1989). In the latter half of the twentieth century, untrammeled faith in scientific progress seems unwarranted. The ability to alter our physical environment is causing life-threatening changes in our ecosphere; the control of disease is more elusive than ever as pandemics outstrip medical solutions; economic inequality is causing widening social divisions; and social supports are becoming increasingly tenuous.

While not all these effects can be laid on the doorstep of scientific research, the profound impact of scientifically based values has had a wide-reaching impact on popular consciousness.

At the same time that these challenges are being raised, and perhaps because of them, counter-developments have been emerging as hopeful antidotes to an unbridled commitment to a modern, scientific world view. Burgeoning literature in fields as diverse as anthropology, psychology, physics, biochemistry, human development, health and ecology have produced intellectual reverberations against the prevailing assumptions about the world as we know it. One consequence of this fervor has been the development of ideas representing a definite departure from foundation-based principles of the modern world and the creation of a postmodern or post-positivist outlook for the coming century. The postmodern world, difficult to carefully define, seems to be evolving as one in which many voices struggle to be heard, in which many perspectives daily pass insistently before our eyes, in which any notion of an inviolable or singular truth is more accurately seen as truth in trouble (Gergen, 1991). Robert Jay Lifton (1993) asserts that we are becoming fluid and many-sided . . . evolving a sense of self appropriate to the restlessness and flux of our time (p. 1). In the face of this fluidity, however, the self remains resilient, changing standpoints, as it must, to meet the mutable demands and experiences of everyday life, drawing upon a heretofore unimagined array of capacities, ingenuities, and resources. It is now more incumbent upon us, in this postmodern world, however we might resist, to embrace a plurality of points of view, to abdicate totalizing discourse (Gergen, 1991), to opt for relevance not rigor (Schon, 1983), and to understand that most realities are products of human relationships, discourse, and meaning-making rather than the revelations of the scientific method (Bruner, 1990). We believe that the strengths perspective in social work and the supporting perspectives from other fields reflect these new understandings.

THE SUBMERGED AND POSTMODERN PERSPECTIVES

Not unlike other professions and disciplines in this time of flux and uncertainty, social work finds itself discovering and rediscovering, developing and redeveloping orientations, ideas, and appreciations that will markedly change the way it goes about professional knowing and doing. There are some persistent themes in these constructs and frameworks that revive and reinforce social work conceptions, beliefs, and values including:

1. Every individual, group, family and community has assets and resources to be used in reconstructing and redirecting their lives.
2. Every individual and collectivity has the inherent capacity for wholeness, regeneration, healing and transformation.
3. Every person and group has a fund of innate wisdom and health to draw upon in times of crisis and challenge.
4. Everyone has the capacity for rebound and righting the trajectory of their development in the face of adversity and trauma.
5. All individuals, families, communities, and cultures have rhetorical, metaphorical, narrative tools to refashion and reformulate their understanding and interpretation of their situation and condition.

All of these themes have roots in social work traditions and history, although some modernist perspectives have, to a degree, obscured them. Developments in social work and related fields are calling these themes back into awareness.

THE STRENGTHS PERSPECTIVES IN SOCIAL WORK

The approach to practice now being called the strengths perspective (Sullivan & Rapp, 1994; Saleebey, 1992, 1995; Weick, 1989, 1992) is based on one of the earliest creeds of social work: build on people's strengths. Mary Richmond (1917) referred to people's latent possibilities (p. 29) and later wrote: ". . . individuals have wills and purposes of their own and are not fitted to play a passive part of the world" (1922, p. 22). This theme was carried forward through the years by such writers as Bertha Reynolds (1932), who cautioned social workers to weigh soberly the strength of natural forces and who encouraged them to mobilize the resources within and without (p. 17) and by Ruth Smalley (1967), who identified as the purpose of social work: to release human power in individuals for personal fulfillment and social good and to release social power for the creation of the kinds of society, social institutions and social policy which make self-realization possible for all (p. 1). The language of latent possibilities, the strength of natural forces, and human power all point to a deep reverence for the inherent capacity of human beings to grow in ways that are transformative. This represents an understanding of the process of change which highlights essential human capacity. There is no intimation that such change is easy or automatic. On the contrary, these authors recognize the complexities both within and without which challenge this naturally-occurring growth process. However, the strengths perspective asserts a fundamental premise: that it will be through the mobilization and articulation of inherent talents, abilities, aspirations, resources, wiles and grit that transformation, rebound, and change will occur. It is these native capacities, individual and collective, that merit the dignity and respect to which each human being is entitled.

The strengths orientation requires a different way of regarding individuals, families, and communities. All must be seen in the light of their capacities, competencies, possibilities, visions, values, hopes, no matter how deformed or dashed these may have become through contingency, injustice, or trauma. In a strengths approach we are obliged to make an accounting of what people know and what they can do. We are beholden to render a roster of resources that exist within and around individual, family, and community. It takes courage and a degree of trust for a social worker to look through this lens. Such a re-vision demands that we suspend initial disbelief in our clients. Too often we are unprepared to hear and believe what clients tell us and what their particular stories might be (Lee, 1994). This is especially true if they have engaged in destructive, abusive, addictive, or wanton behavior.

It is also important for us to realize that the bureaucracy and organization of helping, the methods of inquiry, and the pedagogy of social work are sometimes anathema to appreciating and employing the strengths of people and groups. In too many formal and informal venues of helping, education, and research, the operative vocabulary obscures the language and lexicon of those we seek to help. Pursuing a practice based on the ideas of resilience, rebound, and possibility, is difficult because some of social work's historical and durable beliefs and values have become submerged by modernist views. To make these observations is not to diminish and overlook the real agony and anguish that individuals have faced, either as children or adults; nor is it to deny the reality of violation of so many children; neither is it to deny the clutch and thrall of addictions and how they can morally and physically swamp the spirit of individuals. But it is to deny the presumptuous dominion of various scientifically derived categorical imperatives, whether civic, medical, or moral. It is to deny that people who face distress and injury, even catastrophe, inevitably are wounded, incapacitated or become less than they might. It is to deny that we can assist others by ignoring the possibilities in their lifeworld: stories and narratives; values and beliefs; informal, natural resources; visions and hopes; abilities and gifts, cultural lore and lessons.

At first glance, the resurrection of traditional value principles in social work, while laudable, may seem transparent. Few social workers would challenge their importance. However the strengths perspective in fundamental ways changes the modernist heritage of psychopathology and problem-solving which has permeated social work practice for a significant part of this century. Over the course of much of the profession's development, the alliance with conceptual and theoretical frameworks has made these classical values all but invisible in practical terms. If theory has been borrowed from, or built upon, the social sciences, disciplines which explicitly strive to remove value considerations and consequences from their studies, and through clinical theory primarily concerned with understanding human flaw and frailty, then it indeed will be a sobering task to build an approach to practice that builds on people's strengths. How do we recognize and lay claim to this domain when there is little recognition that it even exists? For over a century, research has largely focused on the glass half empty. The DSM-IV is a symbol of this emphasis, with its 600 pages of entries on human deficiencies, defects, and foibles. To examine the strengths and resiliencies of people in their everyday lives signals, once again, an important shift in our thinking.

A focus on strengths must be a conscious strategy for restoring the submerged value tradition of social work. As one avenue for refreshing practice, the strengths perspective aligns us both with the value base of our profession and with a larger postmodern movement. The kinship of the strengths perspective with emergent thinking, inquiry, and practice in human development offers interesting evidence that social work's early insights about people's inherent capacity for positive metamorphosis are now at the edge of theory development about the nature of human capacities.

RESILIENCE AND THE MIND/BODY CONNECTION

The research and writing in the varied fields that are developing a new story about human capacity began with attempts to understand the developmental course of children who had been confronted with persistent, intense, or sudden overwhelming stress and hardship. What researchers in a variety of disciplines quickly discovered was that a simple accounting of the risk factors faced by these children was not very predictive of outcomes for them in adolescence and adulthood (Garmezy, 1994; Rutter, 1985). Rather, how children developed and thrived depended on at least one other set of factors—those elements in the environment that seemed to provide a protective belt around these children, cushioning the effect of environmental distress, and encouraging rebound and growth (Masten, 1994; Garmezy, 1994). More recently, there has been talk of another set of factors that we might call generative. These are remarkable, fortuitous, and revelatory factors that cumulatively, dramatically and exponentially increase learning, hardiness, resourcefulness, and rebound (Saleebey, 1995; Rutter, 1985).

One of the virtues of the resilience literature, from a social work point of view, is that it thrusts us conceptually into the elegant, complex interplay between person and environment, a claim social work has traditionally staked out for itself. Likewise, it situates our concern immediately in the accounting of assets and capacities, as well as risks and liabilities. This growing body of knowledge is a likely candidate to replace social work educators' continuing romance with stage theories of development, theories that, to a considerable degree, are focused on emergent pathology, and often ignore the antic and fortuitous interaction of political, social, and cultural factors in the lives of individuals, families and communities, not to mention disregarding the bounty and capital existing within individuals and communities. Furthermore, among the factors thought to make people(s) resilient are the character of the constructions, often collective, they build in the face of presumed adversity.

Whatever other conclusions one might draw from the resilience research, one that comes blaring through the din of data and conceptualization is that rebound from and the surmounting of trauma, privation, abuse, and adversity is the rule, not the exception. Resilience is the gathering and development of capacities, wisdom, skills, perspective, and attitudes that make one more capable of meeting life's challenges. Resilience is not the blithe ignoring of one's difficult life situations or the denial of one's pains and wounds. It is, rather, the determination to go on with life in spite of one's scars. It is the capacity to have learned from adversity and to make life decisions on the basis of that learning (Wolin & Wolin, 1993). Thus, for many individuals the ordeals of life have turned out to be instructive and illuminating.

Communities play a part in the development of resilience in individuals and families. Those communities that seem to amplify resilience acknowledge and employ the assets of their members. A widespread ethos of involvement and participation exists (Kretzmann & McKnight, 1993; Benard, 1994). In such communities, neighborhoods, and social spaces, individuals are known for what they do and know and are encouraged to become more competent and knowledgeable. In these communities, many ways are available for individuals and families to make contributions to the moral and civic life of the community and take on the role of full-fledged citizens (Kretzmann & McKnight, 1993; Montuori & Conti, 1993). In discussing the often neglected role of youth in any community, Benard (1994) suggests that youth in trouble can often be sent down a very different path if the community provides three things: the caring of competent and credible mentors and other adults; high, positive, and attainable expectations of them; and opportunities to participate and to do well, and to contribute to the vitality of communal life. Roger Mills (1994), using very similar principles, has helped many very troubled and anomic communities turn from dispiritedness, danger, and insecurity toward a more vibrant, interactive, and productive communal life. In this research and work one thing becomes absolutely clear: there is a transforming interaction between community development, group empowerment, and individual resilience.

Illustrating many of these ideas is the celebrated longitudinal study of at-risk children on the island of Kauai, Hawaii. Begun in 1955, Emmy Werner and Ruth Smith, the principal investigators, reported in 1982 that one out of every three children who, by a variety of measures, were judged to be at risk for a number of adolescent problems turned out to be confident and competent youth at age 18. In their follow-up study, Werner and Smith (1992) discovered that two out of three of the remaining two-thirds had evolved into caring and efficacious adults at age 32. One of the central ideas of these studies is that all individuals have self-righting tendencies and if we can identify some of the factors that alter the developmental trajectory perhaps, in policy and practice, we can capitalize on them. For example, one of the factors that Werner and Smith (1992) observed was the presence of an adult or a peer who was steadfast and caring. Similarly, from his own longitudinal studies, and on the findings of others, Vaillant (1993) concludes that the transformative powers of the self, the capacity of the ego for healthy metamorphosis in the face of pain, even catastrophe, is both remarkable and inherent, and related as well to the character of the community.

HEALTH AND REGENERATION

A new understanding of the body is emerging which supports a postmodern focus for practice. The outburst of evidence of the remarkable generative and renewable powers of the body draws our attention to the inherent organismic push toward wholeness and wellness. Murphy (1993) says it well:

[We] have unprecedented access now to evidence for human transformative capacity. . . . In this multidisciplinary organization of knowledge, we can draw upon the physical, biological,

and human sciences, including new fields such as psychoneu-
roimmunology, that are revealing human nature's capacity for
creative change. (p. 23)

Illustrating Murphy's contention, there is also now an incipient
view of the brain suggesting that over evolutionary time, it has
become an amazing array of neuronal modules (relationships
between neuronal tracts) that underlie innumerable behaviors and
capacities. In a sense, we already know what we need to know in
order to survive. That is, at some level the environment selects from
our inherent, inchoate capacities (underwritten by the aforemen-
tioned modules), those behaviors, cognitions, and emotions needed
to adapt, adjust, and develop. Learning, of course, elaborates and
refines or suppresses these indigenous potentials (Gazzaniga,
1992). For a postmodern orientation to strengths, this means that
there is, in some ways, a congenital propensity to surmount and
survive. There really is, then, an innate wisdom of the body upon
which we can and do draw. It can be thwarted or suppressed by any
number of social, political, cultural, physical factors, but our potential for transformation and bouncing back is in our genes.

Other germinating notions about the fabulous and ornate interaction between body, mind, and environment suggest the vigorous
restorative powers of the self. Life-affirming beliefs, the support of
others, a caring environment, positive emotions, and a sense of
control over, and decisiveness about, one's fate are among the factors (Cousins, 1989; Dossey, 1994) that render the body a most
effective health maintenance organization (Ornstein & Sobel, 1987,
p. 36). There is an increasingly intelligible relationship between
individual resilience and health, and the community surround. The
health realization/community empowerment movement is a powerful testament to this (Mills, 1994). People do have innate wisdom
and resilience, although it may be obscured by oppression, poverty,
and attacks on self-esteem. If resilience, as evidenced by the drive
to health, wisdom, and motivation are, in some ways, intrinsic, and
if they are directly accessible to education and support, then they
can be converted into resources that enhance community vitality.
Likewise, those communities that invite participation, high positive
expectations of its members, and networks of caring people can tap

into the inborn capacities of every individual. The idea, then, is to reconnect people to the health in themselves and then direct them in ways to bring forth the health of others [in the community]. The result is a change in people and communities which builds up from within rather than [being] imposed from without (Mills, cited in Benard, 1994, p. 22).

The resilience and body/mind/environment literature run parallel in many regards. Both imply that individuals and communities have intrinsic capacities for restoration and rebound. Both suggest that individuals are best served, from a health and competence standpoint, by creating belief and thinking around possibility and values, around accomplishment and renewal, rather than centering exclusively on risk factors, disease processes, and problems. Both indicate that health and resilience are, in the end, community projects, an effect of social connection, the aggregating of collective vision, the mobilizing of individual strengths, the provision of mentoring, and the reality of belonging to an organic whole. Finally, the buoyancy of any individual or community depends on the availability, vitality, and recognition by others of their own systems of meaning and folk wisdom.

PRINCIPLES FOR REVITALIZING PRACTICE

In light of the research from such fields as biology, health and human behavior, there is increasing evidence that the human potential for growth and well-being is establishing new possibilities for social work practice. In contrast to the foundational assumptions of the modern and medieval world views, where the discoverable world is out there, the essence of postmodernism is its focus on process, relations, plurality, transformation and meaning-making. It begins with the notion that human beings can only make sense of the external world through mediated processes, neurochemical, linguistic, symbolic, and social. The world is, to use James's (1984) phrase, "a blooming, buzzing confusion," until language and culture put it into identifiable shapes. The meanings of those shapes are constructed through social processes (Berger and Luckmann, 1967) and are continually renegotiated. Thus, from a postmodern perspective, we live in an interpretive world, using language to query, persuade, and convince others about what we see and hear. Because there are few situations whose meaning is incontrovertibly clear to everyone, our social lives are largely spent in trying to make sense of what is happening to us and negotiating operative meanings with those around us. Such an endeavor characterizes relationships from intimate to professional.

The centrality of process encourages an examination of the nature of the helping process. Social workers are, in practical terms, experts on process. They know how to establish relationships with a wide variety of people needing services. They can survey the environment for material resources and bring those resources together on behalf of clients. They work with great skill in negotiating human systems, whether family, workplace, neighborhood or community, and mobilizing the energies of these entities toward constructive action. They are able to enter other worlds of meaning to offer help. All of these areas of expertise are commonplace among social workers but the knowledge undergirding this expertise is not well-articulated.

What postmodern thinking adds to this age-old tradition of process expertise is a vocabulary for understanding the substance of process. The ability to engage in the process is one thing. But the grasp of the metaphysics of process is another. One crucial aspect of the philosophy of process which postmodern approaches call into question is what critical thinkers such as Foucault (1980) identify as knowledge-power dimensions. In the modernist conception of practice, professionals are thought to be imbued with expert knowledge about the human condition which usually institutes an explicit power inequality between worker and client. The expert who holds this knowledge, whether social worker, nurse or physician, is seen to be in a socially and morally superior position to the person needing assistance. In this way, forcing clients to disavow the context of their experiential world turns them into specimens to be examined for evidence of pathology. Foucault (1980) concluded that the institutionalized discourse of professions constructs power through an ideology of normalization. To define what is normal immediately creates a denigrated category called abnormal. Attempting to define what is abnormal invites the medicalization and categorization of what are essentially natural and indigenous behaviors. Thus, there is at the core of this model permanent inequality (Miller, 1976).

In a postmodern approach, professional or disciplinary knowledge is not privileged. That is, it is not given a superordinate position over clients' knowledge. To the contrary, a person's knowledge of his or her experience (local knowledge) is viewed as an essential element of the work. In order to understand a human situation, one must go to the actors themselves. The act of telling their stories becomes the focus of work. These stories are not to be diminished by the imposition of categories from the external world. Diagnostic labels, for example, as a primary form of categorization, are a means to reinterpret people's reality and take control of their story in ways that generally reduce their sense of competence and confidence. In a postmodern approach, professionals bring their own knowledge to the helping situation but that knowledge is not accorded more authority than the person's own knowledge. Rather, the social worker's investment in process is to assist people in identifying resources and opportunities which may have been hidden from them. In this view, a social work relationship is a partnership, with each party bringing something of value to the transaction. A postmodern view emphasizes the ideas of process, plurality (of knowledge and voice), and the relational quality of knowledge.

The strengths perspective, supported by similar thinking in other fields, exemplifies this line of thinking about the nature of social work practice. It assumes that people, no matter what their circumstances, have significant resources both within and around to grow and transform themselves. Because social workers are experts in process, they help focus these resources to best assist people in accomplishing their goals. The worker does not presume to know the direction to take. There is uncertainty about outcomes, a fact that flies in the face of modernist ideas about cause and effect. Rather, the principle of indeterminacy, borrowed from the field of quantum physics (Wolfe, 1989) suggests the fluid, recursive and non-determined way that human situations unfold.

A postmodern view, as represented by the strengths perspective, rests on a profound belief in people's abilities and an intense focusing by the social worker on uncovering, naming, embellishing and celebrating those abilities, talents and aspirations in service of the desired change. Jerome Frank (1974) and E. Fuller Torrey (1986) have written about the importance to healing of the practitioner's belief in a person's ability to be well, and the client's belief in the efficacy of the practitioner. This premise has become an essential aspect of postmodern efforts to incorporate aspects of healing in both health care and related helping professions (Weil, 1995). The power of the helper's belief may ultimately be the most salient feature of a successful helping process.

CONCLUSION

The principles which spur a postmodern approach to inquiry and practice can be a source for reawakening some of our most profound insights about the nature of professional practice. Within social work, for example, the strengths perspective is, at its heart, a postmodern approach to practice. It allows the value base of the profession to become the most prominent feature of practice by according it the credentials of contemporary research and scholarship on how human beings grow and change. In doing so, it upends modernist assumptions about the nature of practice. The vested knowledge of the practitioners, with its attendant premises of objectivity, rational problem-solving and the elimination of value considerations, all slide from view. Instead, the strengths perspective highlights the values of human potential, engagement of optimistic beliefs, and energetic, involved collaboration in service of human transformation. Without values, our efforts to understand and help are distorted. The eminent developmental psychologist Jerome Kagan (1994) put it this way, "facts alone cannot support a moral proposition. Facts may prune the tree of morality; they cannot be its seedbed" (p. 260).

The centrality of strengths to a reinvigorated view of social work practice is supported, as we have argued, by related developments in virtually every field of inquiry. Rather than borrowing assumptions and methods from other disciplines that deflect or ignore our value commitments, postmodern perspectives can light up and amplify our most essential understandings about human well-being and the social good. The result is a value-compatible approach to practice, where our appreciations of human capacity and social resources in the context of process and relationship become the direct focus of our inquiry and practice. What had once been submerged can now enjoy the energy of our curiosity, passion and purpose. Whether it is pursuing a strengths perspective or other like developments in social work, we will see that our work is part of a larger intellectual landscape where head and heart form a new relationship. In moving beyond modernism, we may indeed discover the wise and deeply moral seedbed that has been with social work all along.

REFERENCES

Benard, B. (1994). *Applications of resilience: Possibilities and promise.* Paper presented at a conference on the role of resilience in drug abuse, alcohol abuse, and mental illness. Washington, DC: National Institute on Drug Abuse.

Berger, P. & Luckmann, (1967). *The social construction of reality.* Garden City, NY: Doubleday.

Berman, M. (1989). *Coming to our senses: Body and spirit in the hidden history of the West.* New York: Simon & Schuster.

Bruner, J. (1990). *Acts of meaning.* Cambridge, MA: Harvard University Press.

Cousins, N. (1989). *Head first: The biology of hope.* New York: W.W. Norton.

Dossey, L. (1994). *Healing words: The practice of prayer and the practice of medicine.* San Francisco: Harper San Francisco.

Fischer, J. (1981). The social work revolution. *Social Work,* 26, 199-207.

Frank, J. (1974). *Persuasion and healing.* New York: Schocken Books.

Foucault, M. (1980). *Power/Knowledge: Selected interviews and other writings, 1972-1977.* New York: Pantheon.

Gazzaniga, M. (1992). *Nature's mind: The biological roots of thinking, emotion, sexuality, language, and intelligence.* New York: Basic Books.

Garmezy, N. (1994). Reflections and commentary on risk, resilience, and development. In R. J. Haggerty, L. R. Sherrod, N. Garmezy & M. Rutter (eds.). *Stress, risk, and resilience in children and adolescence: Processes, mechanisms, and interventions.* New York: Cambridge University Press.

Gergen, K. (1991). *The saturated self.* New York: Basic Books.

Goldstein, H. (1986). Toward the integration of theory and practice: A humanistic approach. *Social Work,* 31, 352-357.

Grinnell, R. et al. (1995). Social work researcher's quest for respectability. *Social Work,* 39 (4), 469-470.

Hudson, W. (1982). Scientific imperatives in social work research and practice. *Social Service Review,* 56, 246-258.

James, W. (1984). *Psychology: Briefer course.* Cambridge, MA: Harvard University Press.

Kagan, J. (1994). *Galen's prophecy: Temperament in human nature.* New York: Basic Books.

Kretzmann, J. P. & McKnight, J. L. (1993). *Building communities from the inside out.* Evanston, IL: Center for Urban Affairs and Policy Research, Northwestern University.

Lee, J. A. B. (1994). *The empowerment approach to social work practice.* New York: Columbia University Press.

Lifton, R. J. (1993). *The protean self: Human resilience in an age of fragmentation.* New York: Basic Books.

Masten, A. N. (1994). Resilience in individual development: Successful adaptation despite risk and adversity. In M. C. Wang & E. W. Gordon (eds.). *Educational resilience in inner-city America: Challenges and prospects.* Hillsdale, NJ: Lawrence Erlbaum.

Miller, J. B. (1976). *Toward a new psychology of women.* Boston: Beacon.

Mills, R. (1994). *Realizing mental health.* New York: Sulzburger & Graham.

Montuori, A. & Conti, I. (1993). *From power to partnership: Creating the future of love, work, and community.* United Kingdom: HarperCollins.

Murphy, M. (1993). *The future of the body: Explorations into the further evolution of human nature.* New York: Tarcher/Perigee Books.

Ornstein, R. & Sobel, D. (1987). *The healing brain.* New York: Simon & Schuster.

Randall, J. H. (1976). *The making of the modern mind.* New York: Columbia University Press.

Reynolds, B. (1932). A changing psychology in social casework–after one year. *The Family,* June, 107-111.

Reynolds, B. (1942). *Learning and teaching in the practice of social work.* New York: Farrar & Rinehart.

Richmond, M. (1917). *Social diagnosis.* New York: Russell Sage Foundation.

Richmond, M. (1922). *What is social casework?* New York: Russell Sage Foundation.

Rifkin, J. (1985). *Declaration of a heretic.* London: Routledge & Kegan Paul.

Rosaldo, R. (1989). *Culture and truth: The remaking of social analysis.* Boston: Beacon Press.

Rutter, M. (1985). Resilience in the face of adversity: Protective factors and resistance to psychiatric disorder. *British Journal of Psychiatry,* 147, 598-611.

Saleebey, D. (1993). Theory and the generation and subversion of knowledge. *Journal of Sociology & Social Welfare,* 20 (1), 5-26.

Saleebey, D. (ed.) (1992). *The strengths perspective in social work practice.* White Plains, NY: Longman.

Saleebey, D. (in press). The strengths perspective in social work practice: Extensions and cautions. *Social Work.*

Schon, D. A. (1983). *The reflective practitioner.* New York: Basic Books.

Smalley, R. (1967). *Theory for social work practice.* New York: Columbia University Press.

Sullivan, W. P. & Rapp, C.A. (1994). Breaking away: The potential and promise of a strengths-based approach to social work practice. In R. G. Meinert, J. T. Pardeck & W. P. Sullivan (eds.). *Issues in social work: A critical analysis.* Westport, CT: Auburn House.

Task Force on Social Work Research. (1991). *Building social work knowledge for effective services and practice*. NIMH.

Torrey, E. F. (1986). *Witchdoctors and psychiatrists*. Northvale, NJ: Jason Aronson.

Tyson, K. (1995). *New foundations for scientific social and behavioral research: The heuristic paradigm*. Boston: Allyn & Bacon.

Vaillant, G. E. (1993). *The wisdom of the ego*. Cambridge, MA: Harvard University Press.

Weick, A. (1987). Beyond empiricism: Toward a holistic conception of social work. *Social Thought*, 13 (4), 36-46.

Weick, A. et al. (1989). A strengths perspective for social work practice. *Social Work*, 34, 350-354.

Weick, A. (1991). The place of science in social work. *Journal of Sociology & Social Welfare*, 18, 13-34.

Weick, A. (1992). Building a strengths perspective for social work. In D. Saleebey (ed.). *The strengths perspective in social work practice*. White Plains, NY: Longman.

Weil, A. (1995). *Spontaneous healing*. New York: Alfred A. Knopf.

Werner, E. & Smith, R. (1992). *Overcoming the odds*. Ithaca, NY: Cornell University Press.

Wolfe, F. A. (1989). *Taking the quantum leap*. New York: Harper & Row.

Wolin, S. J. & Wolin, S. (1993). *The resilient self: How survivors of troubled families rise above adversity*. New York: Villard.

Consequences
for Professional Social Work
Under Conditions of Postmodernity

Roland Meinert

SUMMARY. The philosophical perspective of postmodernism is gaining rapid acceptance throughout social work practice and education. In the past few years the social work literature is uniform and consistent in describing its alleged advantages and relevance. This article takes the position that the acceptance of postmodernism by social work has taken place in uncritical fashion. It examines and discusses postmodernism and some potential unintended and negative consequences of it. *[Article copies available for a fee from The Haworth Document Delivery Service: 1-800-342-9678. E-mail address: getinfo@haworth.com]*

The influence of postmodernism is now strongly evident throughout the entire profession of social work following its appearance several decades ago within the literary, natural science, artistic and social science fields. The increase of articles in social work journals attests to the extent to which postmodernism is beginning to enter the collective conscience of the profession. In some quarters it is being argued that postmodernism when allied with the intellectually compatible movement of feminism will constitute a new paradig-

Roland Meinert, PhD, is President of the Missouri Association for Social Welfare, Jefferson City, MO 65101.

[Haworth co-indexing entry note]: "Consequences for Professional Social Work Under Conditions of Postmodernity." Meinert, Roland. Co-published simultaneously in *Social Thought* (The Haworth Pastoral Press, an imprint of The Haworth Press, Inc.) Vol. 18, No. 3, 1998, pp. 41-54; and: *Postmodernism, Religion and the Future of Social Work* (ed: Roland G. Meinert, John T. Pardeck, and John W. Murphy) The Haworth Pastoral Press, an imprint of The Haworth Press, Inc., 1998, pp. 41-54. Single or multiple copies of this article are available for a fee from The Haworth Document Delivery Service [1-800-342-9678, 9:00 a.m. - 5:00 p.m. (EST). E-mail address: getinfo@haworth.com].

41

matic conceptual and philosophical foundation for the profession. If true, then after postmodern beliefs are crystallized and incorporated into the ethos of professional social work then the manner in which its members practice their craft will be significantly and unalterably different than it is now.

To date, the critical mass of postmodern discussion in social work has moved in the direction that promotes what its advocates see as a more valid and realistic organizing framework for day-to-day practice. Indeed, given the characteristics of contemporary social work and the absence in the larger society of a consensus about its mission and purpose, the postmodern approach with its emphasis on uncertainty and indeterminacy provides a comfortable fit. It is reasonable to conclude that if postmodernism did not exist then social work would have to invent it as a philosophical foundation for a profession lacking a definitive intellectual and theoretical compass. What the literature discussion lacks, however, is a full explication of the essential elements of postmodernism and an incisive examination of their potential negative consequences for social work. It is these dimensions of the postmodern movement in social work that this article examines. It will be argued that social work now very much mirrors contemporary society and includes its salient characteristics of chaos, indeterminacy, rampant subjectivism and disdain for reason and traditional science.

In this article the intent is to demonstrate that many of the central elements of the postmodern position have not been fully examined in the social work literature, and that when they are subjected to critical analysis it portends more negative rather than positive consequences for the profession. The effects of these consequences are examined in areas affecting social work practice, the arena of social policy, social work education and the accreditation of social work education programs.

POSTMODERN EMPHASIS IN SOCIAL WORK

The social work journal literature in the recent past demonstrates an increase in articles arguing for postmodernism as a framework for understanding the central issues facing the profession and for organizing general practitioner behavior. This literature reveals several trends. First, the authors appear to select for readers the salient postmodern positions that appear to have relevance to professional social work as it now exists. Second, it promotes and advocates the utility of these positions for social work practice in a persuasive fashion while at the same time leaving unexamined their negative consequences and disutility. Last, the articles do not identify and fully examine the postmodern positions that appear to be illogical or even nonexistent in the daily lives of social work clients or that are relevant to social policy issues. In this last regard, some of the features of postmodernism represent abstract philosophical musings having nothing at all to do with the full range of human experience or the issues faced by social work practitioners and social policy developers. Therefore, it is important for the discussion that follows to selectively identify some of the more salient postmodern positions recently appearing in the social work literature.

Pardeck, Murphy and Choi (1994) advise social workers to adopt the practice stance of not treating the social world and culture as an "objective system." In their view, society, culture and social facts do not exist as traditionally understood in a larger sense but only as they are interpretively defined in a "local" or smaller life space domain. Based on this belief, and logically following from it, social work intervention should not be targeted toward individuals or larger systems but toward communities which comprise a web of linguistically shared meanings. Laird (1995) insightfully ties postmodernism into the family of movements that include deconstructionism, poststructuralism and existentialism. For the social work practitioner this requires a deconstruction of the realities that have been defined by those in positions of social power (social workers) and the recreation of new meanings. Thus, the models, theories, professional educational foci and even professional organizations that have defined how social workers approach practice must be called into question. The traditional process of assessment and measurement by which social workers define problems and seek out solutions would be abandoned according to this view. The concept of expert as knower is to be replaced by enabling clients to acquire the power to be their own diagnostician. She suggests that the concept of the individual or the family as the primary systems of intervention may need to be called into question.

In the clinical field, Pozatek (1994) has examined the fashion in which social workers seek certitude and truth in relation to client problems. She recommends that this be abandoned and replaced by a posture of uncertainty whereby social workers give up their positions of power based on a knowledge which enables them to be the definer of truth. Following Foucault (1980), a main spokesperson for the postmodern approach, she defines truth and power as the same thing. In clinical situations she feels clients are in marginalized positions vis-à-vis the helper who can best help them by restoring power to clients who will develop their own truth meanings and determine the subsequent course of intervention. Hartman (1992), a nationally recognized spokesperson for social work, writes along the same theme by stating that professions develop "global unitary knowledges" which gives them power over clients. In her view, this leads to denial of the "subjugated knowledges" which arise out of the local and indigenous knowledge of clients who are located at the margins of society. Hartman touches upon but does not offer solutions for the dilemma facing social workers who are asked to give up the knowledge gained in their professional training for the localized and subjugated knowledge at the margins.

In writing about social work in both England and the United States, Parton (1994) depicts the profession as undergoing fundamental changes as it moves beyond the era of modernity. The basic principles of modernity which helped define social work included the use of reason as a basis for practice, the development of universal categories of experience and the belief in the generalizability of knowledge. It was these deterministic principles, as well as others, that provided the conceptual building blocks for the modern welfare state. In his view, postmodernism is not only antagonistic toward the attributes of social work modernity, but in large measure rejects their relevance and utility. The pursuit of order and control, calculability, belief in science, rationality and progress are being replaced by the postmodern attributes of social pluralism, indeterminacy and distrust of science and progress through rational planning. Whereas social work under conditions of modernity enabled judgments to be made within some professional rules and guidelines in the postmodern period, they are made in the absence of fixed rules. In Parton's view, social work has become a profession shrouded in uncertainty, without a fixed conceptual and theoretical compass, which post-modernism is attempting to fill.

Given the demise of modernity as a backdrop for social work and the emergence and acceptance of postmodernity, Weick (1993) advocates a complete restructuring of social work education. She sees a paradox in social work education having created a knowledge base for itself which is located outside the reality constructed by the clients that are to be served. If knowledge is the product of mediation and interpretation via the process of language between social worker and client, a constructed knowledge, then the traditional use of the scientific model (technical rationality) is invalid. The postmodern view of knowledge which denies objective reality and emphasizes instead knowledge as a process that is contextually created and recreated is the obverse of the long-standing social work adherence to logical positivism and the scientific method.

FEMINISM AND POSTMODERNISM

The intellectual connection between feminist theory and post-modernism has been articulated by Sands and Nuccio (1992). In their view, there are at least four ways in which they are related. The first is the belief that women view reality from a perspective that is different from that of men, relying more on intuition and subjectivity than reason and objectivity. Because of this difference they will approach science not in the traditional logical positivist manner, seen as a male approach, but in a more subjective fashion. One feminist view is that traditional masculine science attempts to dominate, subdue and penetrate the secrets of nature and because of this it is intrinsically destructive. By contrast science as practiced by women is centered on context, subjectivity and relationships and because of this is intrinsically more humane. Second, feminists eschew the search for categories of knowledge in favor of seeking out truth in a more contextual and situational mode. Thus, the most important reality is that which is local and defined by the participants in smaller groups rather than the larger society. Third, because of their history of oppression, women will decenter their knowledge-seeking by working more on the margins of society rather than where institutional and political power is located. Last, gender or radical feminists in particular seek to deconstruct the traditional logical positivist model of science and replace it with a method of doing science that is structured by the very context in which the knowledge quest is taking place.

It is risky to discuss a feminist perspective of science and postmodernism as if all women in this movement share identical beliefs. There are many different feminist perspectives and world views. At one end of the spectrum are those who feel women are under a state of siege by society and men and seek solutions that involve radical transformations of institutions and the creation of a new culture. By some these are termed radical feminists. At the other end are those who view themselves as equity feminists who seek solutions and full realization of female capacities by insuring the access for women to enter and maximize the use of existing educational, employment and scientific opportunity structures. It is likely that radical feminists would abandon the traditional methods of science, while equity feminists would adhere to it. Radical feminists and postmodernists want to create a new and transformed method of doing science. Equity feminists want the door opened in order to exercise their talents within traditional scientific methods.

Therefore, a central tenet of radical feminism and a logical extension of postmodernism is that science as practiced by women will be fundamentally different than practiced by men. The feminist and postmodern view of reality is that it is a social construct and not amenable to understanding and explanation by so-called objective and detached (value free) methods. In this regard it is indisputable that in fields in which traditional science is practiced that men outnumber women. There are many explanations for the under-representation of women in traditional science but two stand out. One is that women experience a completely different set of life experiences (socialization) that keep them out of the ongoing situations in which the methods and processes of traditional science are emphasized. If women are not socialized in the ways of traditional science then it is reasonable to assume that they will not be able to access the opportunity structures of it. The second is that women think in a manner that is fundamentally different from that of men which leads them to approach the search for truth in a different way. This is the indeterminate approach to science embedded in the postmodern position. The first view is that women have experiences different from those of men, and the second is that they have different attributes. It is believed that these attributes provide women with a "standpoint" different from men's, leading to ways of knowing that are different. These feminine standpoints, it has been argued, put women at an advantage in conducting science. These standpoints are in conformity with the major tenets of postmodernism.

Many equity feminists dispute the view that in regard to the processes of knowing, understanding reality and practicing science that women have attributes different from men's. For example, Haack (1992) a leading female epistemologist and equity feminist has convincingly debunked the idea that science has a masculine character. She argues that women are just as proficient in mathematics, abstract reasoning, objectivity and rational thinking, the hallmarks of traditional science, as are men. In the absence of evidence to the contrary it must be recognized that women have the same level of cognitive abilities as men. The reality is that there is a history of many barriers of tradition and roles that have prevented women from entering high visibility scientific fields. If this is true, then it is likely that cognitive approaches to science are individually based rather than determined by gender per se. Nevertheless, many radical feminists and postmodernists view science and truth seeking in an identical fashion. This includes the deconstruction of current world views of reality and scientific methods and their replacement by a series of ever changing and idiosyncratic ones. One could reasonably ask if indeed there is a feminist standpoint toward science should there not also be one for political conservatives, senior citizens, Irish Catholics, gays and lesbians, retired academics, etc.

THE ESSENCE OF POSTMODERNISM

Even though the social work journal literature discusses the relevance of postmodernism across many dimensions of the profession, none of the writings has succeeded in providing an unequivocal delineation of its essence and central elements. The only position that all postmodern writers in the social sciences seem to agree on is that the movement defies precise definition. Apparently the proponents who argue most vigorously for postmodernism as the new base upon which to reorganize the profession of social work are unable to acknowledge that it is indefinable. Thus a profession which by definition consists of members who "profess" something would paradoxically be based on a foundation which they admittedly cannot define.

There are as many definitions of postmodernism as there are intellectual language communities since conceptual agreement on a larger scale does not exist. Illustrative of this is a scene in the recent movie *City Slickers* described by Marty (1994-1995). There is an old cowboy, played by actor Jack Palance, who is sick and on his last leg and he is sitting on a boulder next to the city slicker, played by actor Billy Crystal. The old cowboy tells the city slicker that he has found the secret of life. "What is it," the city slicker asks. "It is one thing," says the cowboy. "And what is that," asks the city slicker. "That," says the cowboy, "you must decide for yourself." In postmodern terms the scene depicts the belief that one should not embark on a quest for universal truths because only idiosyncratic ones exist.

In understanding the essence of postmodernism it is first necessary to recognize that it is not a theory or a systematic and organized set of conceptual propositions. Even though there are a number of postmodern spokespersons there is a lack of agreement among them on what constitutes its irreducible but necessary central tenets. Basically postmodernism is a set of unorganized assertions about persons and how they perceive and define their world. It is risky, therefore, to attempt an explication of it when no consensual agreement exists, but the attempt must be made in order to further the dialogue about its relevance to social work. The elements and features that appear below appear to be the ones most frequently identified and include those that have implications for understanding the social world and how persons function in it.

Perhaps the major assertion made by postmodernists is the necessity for the individual to escape from the large systems of shared meanings, called metanarratives, which exert a powerful force that must be overcome. It is believed that individuals typically lack the competence and linguistic ability to influence the metanarratives that comprise an oppressive social, economic and political envelope around them. But at the same it is asserted that they possess the competence to operate effectively within a local language community. In the postmodern vision the individual operates in both distal and proximal linguistic environments. In the former, powerful forces dictate how one thinks and acts rendering one communicatively incompetent, while in the latter, by communicative fluency and competence, one can exert control over the immediate environment.

Postmodernists believe that traditional science and the search for truth done within the logical positivist model has resulted in the creation of totalizing metanarratives. This has deflected the truth search away from its rightful and humanly meaningful home which should be within local language communities. Not only should truth be sought at this level but postmodernists draw upon deconstructivist thinking and propose a nihilistic approach to metanarratives. These metanarratives should be torn down or deconstructed in order for the person to escape their oppressively powerful influence. Nihilism and social chaos, while previously viewed as problems, have been redefined by postmodernists into solutions. The process of deconstruction is a central operating principle of both feminists and postmodernists. Deconstruction becomes necessary according to this reasoning since both women and those in local linguistic communities live under conditions of oppression from the larger society which has defined the metanarratives. Not only must the metanarratives be eliminated but they must be replaced by local ones.

Postmodernism is characterized by a pervasive relativism and the elevation of personal freedom and autonomy to the highest order. There are no "social facts" but all facts become equally valid and they are determined locally rather than by those who control the powerful institutions and canons of science. There are no fixed notions of reality as determined by society but only those defined by local linguistic communities. Thus larger "truths" (or metanarratives) do not exist nor are there generally accepted principles and canons by which to seek out truth. Science becomes the process of "literary interpretation." It was Lyotard (1984) who advised a stance of "incredulity" toward all metanarratives because of his belief that all knowledge was grounded in language and interpretation. Those who control the metanarratives have the power to construct reality along their socially preferred lines and postmodernists must become "assassins" of this reality. Theory as conventionally understood becomes obsolete since the social realities they purport to explain are only linguistic fictions. It is difficult to summarize the postmodern position since spokespersons in the main assert more about what they are against than what they favor.

IMPLICATIONS FOR SOCIAL WORK

Those who have advocated for the adoption of the philosophical and conceptual perspective of postmodernism have not examined the negative effects that will appear. These consequences can be critical for both social work as a profession and for social work education as the institution that prepares practitioners. The consequences will not only affect day-to-day practice but will go to the very core and purpose of the profession. If social work is misunderstood by the general public, as is generally thought, then the ambiguity of the postmodern approach is not a positive development. The major implications and consequences of postmodernism for social work are identified and discussed below.

About four decades ago a controversial and widely read article in a popular magazine claimed that social work had lost the bearings upon which it was founded by describing it as a profession that was "chasing its tail" (Sanders, 1957). It argued that psychoanalytic theory had an inordinate influence in schools of social work and on the manner in which professionally trained social workers practiced. Psychoanalysis forced social workers to focus on the intrapsychic (private) troubles of clients that all but blotted out the profession's long-standing commitment to deal with larger social and economic issues. It took social work decades to escape from the clutches of the private trouble orientation dictated by psychoanalysis and return to a focus on larger social problems. A pervasive adoption by social work of a postmodern perspective poses a similar problem by drawing attention away from social realities and inward toward issues of smaller linguistic communities. The several elements of postmodernism that assert that reality and truth only exist within the scope and context of observer participants fit a clinical orientation but not a social change one. Postmodernism suffers from the same theoretical weakness as did psychoanalysis. It is a form of reductionism in that it selects an aspect of reality within the bio-psycho-social-spirituality configuration–the subjective definition of situations–and excludes from consideration all that remains. Psychoanalysis made social workers trained incapacitates in that they were unable to function intellectually outside the realm of the psyche. Postmodernism will force them to focus on only the subjective states existing within smaller communities and close off the objective worlds of social, economic and political reality. By adopting a postmodern philosophy, social work will again return to a state wherein it is "chasing its tail." Postmodern social workers have created an intellectual paradox. On the one hand they assert the postmodern approach is valid while on the other they deny the legitimacy of scientific methods by which their claim to validity could be tested. At this point in the development of postmodernism and its adaptation to social work practice there is no evidence to its worth but only testimonials and exhortations.

Social work has been at the forefront of efforts to define the concept of social justice and to insure that it exists in society. Social justice requires the establishment of a grand "metanarrative" which emerges from societal agreement about the elements and standards that make it up. As an institution social work has specified the basic rights persons have; the basic goods, opportunities and resources all persons need; and the extent of responsibility of sovereign governments to provide them. In postmodern terms these standards constitute an overarching "metanarrative" and in the absence of one there would be as many definitions of social justice as there are linguistic communities. A long-standing assumption in social work is that the profession shares a common set of values which endure over time. They are transmitted to initiates into the profession by both formal education and a socialization process. In a postmodern world these enduring values would not exist since they constitute a "metanarrative" that must be deconstructed and replaced by a series of locally anchored ones. Social justice and a professional value system would become indeterminate concepts residing in many different social work linguistic communities.

It is difficult to see how social work education at all levels would remain unscathed and institutionally stable under postmodern social work. The actual educational process itself and the standards by which programs achieve accreditation would change radically. Currently there exists a set of accreditation standards and a curriculum policy statement which serve as criteria under which both baccalaureate and master's level educational programs are reviewed for accreditation. The standards and statement serve as a "metanarrative" influencing how the several hundred programs organize and structure their educational efforts. In a postmodern profession the standards and statement would first be destroyed (deconstructed) and then replaced by a series of locality defined and interpreted ones. There would be as many standards and statements as there are social work education linguistic communities across the country. Social work education as an institution would be in chaos.

It has been axiomatic for decades that social work education and practice is organized around a knowledge base, a set of core skills and a professional value system. Indeed, the battle fought by social work to achieve "professional" status was predicated on a defense to the assertion that it lacked a systematic knowledge base. Vigorous efforts continue to this day to insure that social services are staffed by professionally trained social workers. Professionally trained assumes the acquisition of a body of knowledge and a set of skills to operationalize it. Yet this assumption is being challenged (Weick, 1993) by the belief that students, social workers and clients exist in a world of their own creation (subjectively defined) while acting as if it was created by powers existing outside them (objective reality). In short, all knowledge is either locally and contextually generated, or it can be generated cross contextually and is generalizable. There are important practice and social policy implications of both these positions. The first believes that conditions such as disability, discrimination, poverty, child abuse, domestic violence, etc. must be locally and contextually defined by those experiencing the condition. The second believes that objective standards can be created by which they can be defined by the larger society. This issue is at the core of the way in which postmodern social work will depart from current practice. Social workers will either believe that objective reality does not exist and practice accordingly, or that it does exist and practice within that epistemological structure. The first dictates practice organized around linguistic communities, and the second around an external and objectively defined reality. In postmodernism there is a farrago of knowledge claims that is different from the view of modernists who work toward a common base.

Social work has been at the forefront in celebrating the value of cultural diversity. At the same time it has emphasized the commonalities shared by all people. Racial and ethnic groups are linguistic communities according to postmodernists and they should be encouraged and supported to define their own realities. However, postmodernism de-emphasizes the universalistic features shared by all. It is difficult to specify, but logical to assume, that postmodern social work will lead to communicative difficulty between groups. When there are an infinite number of small language communities each with discrete rules, patterns and a myriad of idioms, communication within the larger society becomes problematic. By enhancing the power of a variety of linguistic communities the consensual communicative commonalities of the larger society are diminished. The current debate about whether English should be required as an official language illustrates a dilemma for many. Postmodernists would argue against it and promote a multitude of "language games" while traditionalists would seek consensus for a common language.

Admittedly postmodernism presents social work with many intellectually challenging choices. In this regard it is similar to earlier perspectives such as psychoanalysis and systems theory which appeared to offer seductively easy paths to understand complex realities and structure professional practice. However, when both psychoanalysis and systems theory came upon the conceptual scene they were not critically examined for potential negative consequences. The same pattern appears to be taking place with postmodernism in that its value for social work is being touted while consequences of a negative nature remain unexamined. This article has raised questions about the value of postmodernism for social work in several areas, particularly its denigration of traditional science and the elimination of objective social realities in social work. The arguments against postmodernism can be summed up in a story told about Dr. Samuel Johnson. One of his critics insisted that reality did not exist outside of the observer and challenged him to prove otherwise. Dr. Johnson saw a big rock nearby and gave it a vigorous kick. He then said, "I refute it thus."

REFERENCES

Foucault, M. (1980). *Power/knowledge: Selected interviews and other writings, 1972-1977.* Gordon, C. ed., New York: Pantheon Books.

Haack, S. (1992). Science 'from a feminist perspective.' *Philosophy,* 67, 5-18.

Hartman, A. (1992). In search of subjugated knowledge. *Social Work,* 37, 483-484.

Laird, J. (1995). Family-centered practice in the postmodern era. *Families in Society,* 51, 150-162.

Lyotard, J. (1984). *The postmodern condition: A report on knowledge.* Minneapolis: University of Minnesota Press, 11.

Marty, M. (1994/1995). Peers, partners and the nurturing of genius: A century of common cause. *NCA Quarterly,* 69(2/3),

Pardeck, J., Murphy, J. & Choi, J. (1994). Some implications of postmodernism for social work practice. *Social Work,* 39(4), 343-346.

Parton, N. (1994). The nature of social work under conditions of (post)modernity. *Social Work and the Social Sciences,* 5(2), 93-112.

Pozatek, E. (1994). The problem of certainty: Clinical social work in the postmodern era. *Social Work,* 39(4), 396-403.

Sanders, M. (1957). Social work: A profession chasing its tail. *Harpers Magazine,* 214, 56-62.

Sands, R., & Nuccio, K. (1992). Postmodern feminist theory and social work. *Social Work,* 37(6), 489-494.

Weick, A. (1993). Reconstructing social work education. *Journal of Teaching in Social Work,* 8(1/2), 11-30.

The Role of Religious Auspiced Agencies in the Postmodern Era

SUMMARY. On the face of it postmodernism as a philosophy would seem to clash with institutionalized religions and social services provided under religious auspices. Whereas all religions contain a set of beliefs and truths that endure over time, the postmodern position emphasizes beliefs and truths that are contextually anchored and impermanent. The analysis in this paper shows that in relation to social agencies under religious auspices this is not always the case and discusses some of the contextualized aspects of religious social services. *[Article copies available for a fee from The Haworth Document Delivery Service: 1-800-342-9678. E-mail address: getinfo@haworth.com]*

Religious auspiced agencies have been a significant provider of various forms of social and health services in the United States throughout the 20th century. However, as urbanization, the development of the welfare state, and the professionalization of social services increased in the latter half of the century, the roles of religious auspiced agencies have changed. As their roles underwent change, considerable controversy and confusion arose within the broader society and within the churches themselves regarding the appropriateness of these agencies to deliver social services and

---

William J. Hutchison, SJ, PhD, is Associate Professor in the School of Social Services, Saint Louis University, St. Louis, MO 63108.

[Haworth co-indexing entry note]: "The Role of Religious Auspiced Agencies in the Postmodern Era." Hutchison, William J. Co-published simultaneously in *Social Thought* (The Haworth Pastoral Press, an imprint of The Haworth Press, Inc.) Vol. 18, No. 3, 1998, pp. 55-69; and: *Postmodernism, Religion and the Future of Social Work* (ed: Roland G. Meinert, John T. Pardeck, and John W. Murphy) The Haworth Pastoral Press, an imprint of The Haworth Press, Inc., 1998, pp. 55-69. Single or multiple copies of this article are available for a fee from The Haworth Document Delivery Service [1-800-342-9678, 9:00 a.m. - 5:00 p.m. (EST). E-mail address: getinfo@haworth.com].

regarding the appropriate mix of government and voluntary sector activity in the financing and delivery of social services. In the midst of these social, political and economic changes, a new challenge has arisen for religious auspiced agencies in the form of the philosophical and psychological questions posed by a postmodern epistemology. The basic problem raised by postmodernism for religious auspiced agencies can be stated as follows. It appears that religion involves a belief in a set of propositional truths that live over time within the tradition of a religious institution. Postmodernism, on the other hand, involves beliefs that arise out of the way in which an individual person interprets immediate reality. Thus, in social work practice there appears to be an inevitable tension that arises within a practitioner who ascribes to a set of external religious beliefs of his/her religion or of the mission of a religious auspiced agency on the one hand and to an ongoing immediate personal interpretation of reality on the other.

This paper will analyze some of the tensions and challenges posed for religious auspiced agencies that arise both from some of the sociological changes that have occurred during the 20th century and also from the philosophical and psychological perspectives posed by this postmodern epistemology. Since social work is centrally organized around and professes to be concerned about the person in the environment, it is important that the profession critically address these questions. The resolution of some of these dilemmas lies in several sets of distinctions that will be discussed in this paper. The first set of distinctions is the distinction between religion and spirituality. The second distinction is the difference between faith as an intellectual assent to propositional statements and faith conceived as basically a trust in a person. A third set of distinctions is between a strand of religion that grows out of a prophetic tradition of compassion and justice and a strand of religion that grows out of a holiness tradition based on observance of certain behaviors. A fourth distinction is the distinction between religion viewed as a relatively fixed institution and religion viewed as an ongoing search for community.

Central to the thesis of this paper is the view that what lies at the root of the human quest is a search for community based on a compassionate concern for all human persons. Compassion is not limited to any one form of religion but is a characteristic found across many religions and found in persons who ascribe to no formal religion. This view of religion as a search for community based on a compassionate concern for all human persons is close to the view expressed by Pardeck, Murphy and Choi (1994) regarding the proper focus of social work intervention. They persuasively argue that the focus of social work intervention should be neither the individual as such nor systems as such. Rather social work practice should be community based. In their conception of post-modern practice they point out that what they mean by community is a domain where certain assumptions about reality are acknowl-edged to have validity. In their view this reality is linguistically developed and is fragile, as opposed to moral absolutes, but is sufficient to unite people. Since a client's world consists of a web of meanings, created and sustained linguistically, it is essential that a social worker listen and read carefully the meaning attached to the attitudes and behaviors of clients. Effective intervention requires careful listening and interpretation.

Related to the first thesis, which views the root of the human quest as a search for community based on a compassionate concern for all human persons, is the second major thesis of this paper. This thesis includes the belief that in the Judaic-Christian tradition as lived in the United States, church-related agencies are well situated to play a major role in providing compassionate care for vulnerable and poor populations and in advocating on their behalf for policies that make services more affordable and accessible.

DEFINING SPIRITUALITY AND RELIGION

The first set of distinctions that can help understand the tension posed by postmodernism is the distinction between "spirituality" and "religion." Spirituality refers to the dynamic way that a person creates meaning and purpose in life. Its primary focus is on the individual and on the psychological processes by which he/she organizes some type of world view and consciously relates to this world. The concept of relating is a vital part of the concept of spirituality since it focuses on how one connects with other persons in one's environment, how one relates to the physical environment, and, for theists, how one relates to some transcendent other that many conceive as a personal God. There are two things to be noted about this notion of spirituality. The first is that this view of spirituality is neither a denial nor a denigration of the material. Rather its focus is on how a person creates meaning and on the fact that a person is an intentional conscious agent. There are indeed spiritualities that either deny or denigrate the material. However, within many religions there are spiritualities that celebrate the material. One can read the Song of Songs in the Jewish and Christian scriptures for a celebration of the passionate and binding love between a man and a woman. Psalm 104 is a paean of praise for the marvels and beauty of the universe. The second thing to be noted is that spirituality is a dynamic concept. It is assumed that in a healthy mature person spirituality develops over a lifetime.

Religion in this article focuses on an organized, communal expression of a set of beliefs and values and an organized set of rituals and worship that find expression in architecture, painting, music, and dance. Religion also refers to a communal expression of some form of mutual aid and some communal compassionate concern for people and the environment in which they live. Religion also denotes some form of governance and decision making and some set of organized roles for members of a particular religion. When religion is healthy, it nurtures and supports the spiritual development of its adherents. In fact religion is one of the ways that one generation socializes the next generation regarding important beliefs and values and about the ultimate meaning of life. On the other hand, precisely because spirituality and religion are not the same, there is probably always some form of tension that develops at various periods of a person's life between spirituality and religion. A contemporary example that comes to mind of a person with a developed spirituality who found a major tension between his spirituality and his religion is the Scottish philosopher John Macmurray. A veteran of the First World War, he reached a point in his life when he decided that he could no longer in good conscience attend any church because his experience with war and with the churches' close identity with governments brought him to think of the churches as various national religions of Europe (Barry, 1990). A final observation to be made at this juncture is that although religion is concerned about moral issues, it is concerned about more than a moral code. It is concerned about relating to a mystery called God and about foundational attitudes toward all of creation.

THE MEANING OF FAITH

In the earlier definition of religion it was indicated that religion refers to some organized set of beliefs. This is commonly referred to as "faith." Unfortunately, an uncritical approach to faith can lead one to view faith as primarily an assent to propositional statements. However, when most modern theologians examine the notion of biblical faith, they point out that faith is primarily a relational concept that empowers a person to act with conviction instead of resigning oneself to fatalism (Nolan, 1978). To believe is to believe in someone. It is a type of trust that may well lead someone to entrust themselves to someone and to a way of life. In his research on the dynamic of faith over the life cycle, Fowler (1981) points out that one does not pass on one's faith to one's children in the same way that one passes on the family jewels. Rather, maturity, in faith as in every other aspect of human growth and development, entails a personal critical reflection and individualization.

John Haughey (1994), a contemporary theologian, recognizes the challenges that postmodernism presents for any religion. He indicates that postmodernism includes a passion for decoding and deconstructing received meanings while expecting and promoting the development of ever new meanings. With postmodernism, objectivity is out, hermeneutics is in. Truth is neither sought for nor expected since it smacks of dogmatism or group-think. He also goes on to point out that the reason that there is such variation in theologies today is to appreciate the many starting points or sources upon which theologians reflect to understand faith. Some theologians reflect upon scriptures, some upon rituals, some upon the lives of reputed holy or intellectual giants, and some upon contemporary social situations. Social location makes certain texts attractive; it also makes some loyalties more likely than others. Loyalties profoundly affect our interpretations. Our loyalties do not necessarily preclude a critical reading of a text, but they definitely give it a presumption in favor of the loyalty. Weick (1979) makes a similar observation when he says people commonly assert, "I'll believe it when I see it." This bit of wisdom probably should be turned on its ear so that it approximates more closely the way in which people actually act: "I'll see it when I believe it."

It seems reasonable to assume that at least some forms of postmodernism are compatible with faith and with religious expression of one's concern for others. If faith is conceived as a dynamic quest and religion is conceived as a community of people engaged in the quest who preserve the living memory of their predecessor, then there is no reason why deconstruction means that one throws out either the past or any hope that a group of persons can share similar experiences and meanings.

When William James (1990) wrote his classic *The Varieties of Religious Experience* he was insightfully aware that there are many types of religious experience depending upon the personality and the social location of the person having such an experience. A critical approach to one's faith does not mean that one receives the family jewels on the one hand, but neither does it mean that other mature persons do not experience similar patterns of doubt and growth and ways of expressing their religious experience. In an intriguing fashion, Borg (1995) describes his own critical growth in faith. Raised in a Lutheran family in North Dakota he describes his critical religious quest that began in high school when he began "experiencing a collision between the modern world view and his childhood beliefs." By his mid-thirties he had had a number of experiences of what he calls "nature mysticism." These experiences were marked by what Jewish theologian Abraham Heschel (1951) called "radical amazement," moments of transformed perception in which the earth is seen as "filled with the glory of God, shining with a radiant presence" (Heschel, 1951). For Borg these religious experiences were moments of connection in which he felt his linkage to what is and can be. The example of Borg is given to provide a phenomenology of faith as a way of being related to the universe rather than as an assent to propositions. Borg goes on to indicate that this transformation of his understanding of God as the center of existence began to affect his understanding of Jesus as a "Spirit" person, as one whose source of energy was that he was grounded and connected to the world of Spirit. Borg also describes how he came to see the centrality of Jesus' message of compassion as intrinsically related to his life of the Spirit. For Borg there is an intrinsic connection between the boundary-shattering experience of Spirit and the boundary-shattering ethos of compassion. Spirit and compassion go together. However, Jesus was continually a center of controversy among his own religious leaders because his spirituality of compassion was confrontational to the prevailing theology of his day which was a theology of ritual and holiness. For Jesus to mix with and side with persons who were not ritually pure was to run against the primary political paradigm of this purity system. A similar point has been made by Nolan (1978) who describes and discusses the political implications of the life of Jesus. This work opens with an opinion statement describing it as the most accurate and balanced short reconstruction of the life of the historical Jesus. Thus, a reconstructionist approach to religion and spirituality is alive and well in our modern world among theologians as well as among psychologists and philosophers.

In summarized fashion the points that have been covered in this section regarding religion and spirituality include: (1) the maturation process of achieving spirituality requires a critical approach to one's religion; (2) a common experience in a religious conversion is the experience of a mystery as the center of the universe and a personal connectedness to this mystery which many name God. Faith is an existential religious experience, not an assent to some truth that is accepted on the authority of another person. The word of another cannot ground one's faith; (3) in drawing upon the experience of Borg (1995) and of Nolan (1978) it has been emphasized that the conflict that they both acknowledge occurred in the life of Jesus and that seems to be occurring today in many parts of the world between a spirituality that calls one to a concrete compassion for the poor and the vulnerable and institutional paradigms of wealth, power, and oppression; and (4) many modern theologians accept, or at least are comfortable with, the postmodern approach to understanding "reality" as basically a linguistically socially constructed set of meanings that are arrived at only through extensive dialogue and in some historical and community context.

MUTUALITY OF RELIGION AND SPIRITUALITY

In describing the tensions and conflicts that frequently occur between religion and spirituality, one may draw the conclusion that the two are antithetical to each other. Although such may be the case in certain concrete instances, nevertheless, when religion is working well, it is supportive and helpful for spiritual growth. Parents, teachers, and friends can be attractive witnesses to a way of life that one may desire to enter into. Many deeply spiritual persons can point to significant mentors and guides in their own spiritual journey. Even more germane to the present discussion of the role of religious auspiced agencies in a postmodern world is the role that the concept of community can play in providing a medium or a mediating structure for the expression of compassion.

RELIGION AS SUPPORTIVE COMMUNITY

Turning to religion conceived as a form of associational ties to a community, O'Neill (1989) cites several studies that indicate that seventy percent of Americans are members of the nation's 350,000 churches, synagogues, and mosques. Forty percent say that they attend religious services weekly. Over forty million Americans volunteer in religious organizations. In 1987 nearly half of all private funds contributed to charity, about 44 million, was donated to religion. The number of people who donate to religion is more than twice the number who donate to health care, social services, education, or any other charity. As noted by O'Neill (1989) it has been historically documented that many current social service agencies were founded by religious groups. Furthermore, the majority of religious congregations in the United States engage in some form of helping. A 1992 national study found that 92 percent of local congregations were involved in human service activities, 90 percent in health work, 50 percent in arts and cultural activities, 53 percent in education, and 40 percent in environmental efforts (Hodgkinson, Weitzman, & Kirsh, 1993). Furthermore, each of these categories represents a significant increase over a similar survey conducted in 1988 (Hodgkinson, Weitzman, & Kirsh).

It was also found that in 1991 local religious congregations expended or donated $21.1 billion to other than religious activities (Hodgkinson, Weitzman, & Kirsh, 1993). Religious congregations engage in an array of services and provide members and nonmembers with food, clothing, shelter, transportation, counseling, adult education, tutoring, head start, drug prevention programs, community development programs, day care, social and recreational facilities and services, youth group work, senior citizen programs, information and referral services, disaster relief, programs for the handicapped, refugee aid, job training, and legal assistance.

CHURCH RELATED AGENCIES
AS MEDIATING STRUCTURES

The second major thesis of this paper is that church-related agencies are mediating structures within American society that continue to play a vital role in providing direct services and in advocating for more just social policies, i.e., policies that provide more affordability and accessibility to basic human services for poor and vulnerable populations. Many sociologists of religion including Coleman (1982) and O'Neill (1989) conceive of society as composed of three sectors: (1) the government sector; (2) the economic sector; and (3) the independent sector. In Coleman's terminology, they constitute a "mediating" structure vis-à-vis other social arrangements. Following the thought of de Tocqueville, he argues that a healthy democracy is a society that supports and encourages the growth of mediating groups. There is no reason in this scheme of things why religious auspiced agencies should not play a major role in providing basic health, education, and welfare services.

As a matter of empirical fact, church sponsored agencies play a very important role in the provision of these services. In 1991, for example, the Catholic Health Association comprised 1200 Catholic organizations, with 650,000 employees caring for 43 million people a year with a budget of $30 billion (Fahey and Lewis, 1992). In 1993, Catholic Charities comprised 1400 agencies and institutions, with 48,000 employees caring for 10.6 million people with a budget of over $1.9 billion and a volunteer base of nearly 225,000 (Catholic Charities U.S.A., 1994). In 1995, the Evangelical Lutheran Church in America had 245 affiliated social and health ministry agencies with a total budget of $2.4 billion. They employed almost 83,000 persons and had 89,000 volunteers. These agencies served more than 1,868,000 clients (Evangelical Lutheran Church in America, 1995). In 1994 the Salvation Army reported that they employed almost 40,000 persons, used 1.4 million volunteers, provided case work services to more than 11 million persons, served over 1 million youth through boys and girls clubs, and served almost 2 million persons with disaster relief. Their budget that year was over $1.3 billion (The Salvation Army, 1994). The United Methodist Church estimates that in 1994 there were 400 health and welfare agencies affiliated in some way with their organization that served approximately 6 million clients and patients, employed approximately 127,000 full-time persons, and had an annual operating budget of $5.7 billion (United Methodist Church, 1988).

O'Neill (1989) has also pointed out that this third sector, composed of 60,000 social service agencies employing almost a million people, interacts with both the for-profit sector and the government sector in the provision of social welfare. He argues that in the latter two decades of the nineteenth century and the first two decades of the twentieth century, Catholic and Jewish congregations and agencies cumulatively played a much greater role in responding to the needs of America's poor than the host culture nonprofit organizations such as the YMCA, The American Red Cross, and Jane Addams Hull House which have received more attention from historians. He recognizes that by the end of the 1920s there was considerable religious pluralism in America. There were 150 Protestant denominations along with a large population of Catholics (about 20 percent of the population), and approximately 4 million Jews.

The past 40 years have demonstrated that this religious pluralism has not prevented religious auspiced agencies from providing significant human services to tens of millions of Americans. Religious auspiced agencies provided health services funded by Medicare and Medicaid in health facilities constructed under the Hill Burton Act; built and managed housing subsidized by funds from the Department of Housing and Urban Development; provided congregate and home-delivered meals funded under the Older Americans Act;

served refugees with funds from The Refugee Act; and provided residential foster care under contracts for services with a state agency using federal and state funds under Titles IV-B and IV-E of the Social Security Act.

Throughout this article the term "religious auspiced" or "church-sponsored" agency has frequently been used. This term could imply that the major beneficiaries of assistance (i.e., the clients) were persons who are members of the same religious denomination as the administrators and staffs of the agency or of the congregation providing the service. Although this assumption was probably true of the assimilation of immigrants in the early part of the twentieth century, such an assumption is far from obvious today. Today the majority of the clients served and many of the staff and board members of these agencies are no longer of the same denomination as the agency whose name they bear.

In 1991 Fordham University hosted a symposium on the future of Catholic institutional ministries in the three areas of (1) social service; (2) health care; and (3) higher education. The results of this symposium described the historical changes that have taken place in Catholic Charity agencies (Fahey & Lewis, 1992). Originally Catholic social services were not established within diocesan structures but arose in parishes and ethnic communities. It was only after second and third generations of Catholics began to move away from their ethnic roots and traditions that pressures began to build up for federations or associations of Catholic Charities within dioceses. In the ethnic worlds of mutual support the sense of community was much easier to enhance by social services than in the pluralistic modern bureaucracies. The services provided were a natural extension of family, culture and religion.

From 1935 to 1959 Catholic Charities agencies entered an era of professionalization, and after World War II in the mid-1940s these agencies began to move away from a welfare and income maintenance focus to the area of the emerging interpersonal problems of the Catholic middle class. A major shift occurred in 1959 when the federal government introduced "purchase of service" arrangements at the national level as a funding mechanism to solve specific social problems in the local community. This permitted the government to purchase services from voluntary agencies like Catholic Charities to meet public objectives. This policy initiative empowered Catholic Charities agencies to return their service to a focus on the nation's poorest. However, by and large, the poorest were no longer Catholic. With pluralistic work forces, ecumenical boards of directors, public sector and United Way financial support, and a diminished Church-funding base, ambiguity and loss of identity affected the entire Catholic Charities movement during the 1960s. The ambiguity and the openness generated by the Second Vatican Council motivated Catholics in the United States during the late 1960s and early 1970s to rethink the purpose of Catholic Charity agencies. What emerged was a commitment to celebrate their Catholic heritage and yet function in a pluralistic environment by serving three major roles. These included: (1) the provider of quality services to identified needs; (2) advocacy efforts to eliminate the causes of poverty; and (3) convening other groups to address major social problems. This new focus pointed to indications that a religious auspiced agency had several basic models that it could follow: (1) it could be a "sectarian" agency that serves people from its own denomination using personnel and fiscal resources of its own members; (2) it could cease to be a religious auspiced agency and become an independent sector agency with no contemporary religious ties; or (3) it could follow what Joseph Cardinal Bernadin, Archbishop of Chicago, called a "mixed" model with one foot planted in the Church and the other in our pluralistic society (Fahey and Lewis, 1992). In advocating this latter model for Catholic social services, health, and higher education institutions, Cardinal Bernadin recognizes that one must be willing to live with some anxiety as the value systems represented by the church and society may well be in tension.

A similar conclusion was reached by Garland (1994) from her study of child welfare agencies that were founded by various Protestant churches. She observed that the organizational self-perception of religious auspices agencies often changes over time. For the most part, it appears that agencies begin as direct extensions of the church community or religious order and its ministry. As agencies grow and become more sophisticated they come to rely on a professional staff instead of church volunteer workers. However, they also tend to become secularized and identify more closely with the human service network of the community than with the church group that founded them. She recommended that church related agencies embrace their identity as a direct extension of and a leader of the church in its service to the community. To the extent that the agency embraces such a role for itself, effective agency leadership begins with an understanding of the church's mission and how the agency can best guide the church in its response to the needs of children and families. Drawing upon the writings of Alan Keith-Lucas, she points out that a church agency exists as an expression of faith and not to require certain beliefs and behaviors in the people it serves. We call ourselves Christian or Jewish not because of how we insist our clients behave but because of how we behave towards them. Christian or Jewish social work refers to the motivation of the worker, not the motivation of the client. Thus social services are oriented to client needs in the same manner as sectarian agencies.

POSTMODERNISM AND CHURCH RELATED AGENCIES

The preceding discussion regarding the religious roots of many social agencies and the current discussion regarding how these agencies might maintain a religious identity and mission in a pluralistic society is germane to the issue of a postmodern epistemology. Postmodernism does not rule out the possibility that religiously motivated people can continue to serve poor and vulnerable populations and advocate on their behalf. Rather, it rightfully assumes that each generation of religious believers must socially construct the meaning it attaches to its care for others, and it has to both adapt to its culture and also be part of a critical transformation of its society. This point is well expressed by Fahey (1996) who asserts that an analysis of the Catholic identity in Catholic social service agencies must begin with an understanding and appreciation of ambiguity. While one may construct a theoretical framework, the true identity of the agency is socially constructed in a particular time and place by the people who are its stakeholders: boards, administration, workers, clients, the local ordinary, professional organizations, accrediting and licensing agencies, public and private funders, and the Catholic and broader communities in which they function and purport to serve. Additionally, the value structure of society in general and government in particular is also an important influence.

CONCLUSIONS

Throughout the 20th century, religious auspiced agencies have played a major role in providing social and health services to poor and vulnerable groups in society. They have successfully adapted to many sociological, demographic, and economic changes and have advocated on behalf of many social and economic policies that benefit their clients and involve them in the decisions that shape their lives. As they enter the 21st century, many church sponsored agencies are reflecting on their identity and mission. They continue to enunciate a mission of developing compassionate, caring communities and they continue to view themselves as important "mediating" structures in society. They contextualize themselves as part of the not-for-profit sector in society distinct from both the government and the commercial sectors. Many of these agencies are grappling with questions of how to maintain their identity and autonomy even as they relate to and even form alliances with government or commercial sectors. As religious auspiced agencies, they enunciate a spiritual interpretation of reality that views persons as members of communities that provide the type of support and interaction that leads to healthy growth and development. These agencies try to recruit board and staff that share similar values. The mission of these agencies is neither to proselytize clients nor to impose uncritical truth claims upon their staffs. Through dialogue and critical reflection, they take their place in the postmodern era where pluralism is a given and where people respectfully intervene as helping professionals trying to understand the web of relationships that provide meaning both for their clients and for themselves.

REFERENCES

Affiliated Social Ministry Organizations-Evangelical Lutheran Church in America. (1995). 1995 Annual Report. Washington, DC.
Barry, W. (1990). *Now choose life: Conversion as the way of life*. New York: Paulist Press, 65-66.

Borg, M. (1995). *Meeting Jesus again for the first time: The historical Jesus & the heart of contemporary faith*. San Francisco: Harper Collins, 7-14.

Catholic Charities U.S.A. (1994). *The changing signs of the times–1994 annual report*. Alexandria, Virginia.

Coleman, J. (1982) *An american strategic theology*. Ramsey, N.J.: Paulist Press.

Fahey, C. & Lewis, M. (1992). *The future of catholic institutional ministries*. New York: Third Age Center, Fordham University.

Fahey, C. (1996). *The "catholic" in catholic charities*. Alexandria, Virginia: Catholic Charities U.S.A.

Fowler, W. (1981). *Stages of faith*. San Francisco: Harper and Row Publishers.

Garland, D. (1994). *Church agencies*. Washington, DC: Child Welfare League of America.

Haughey, J. (1994). Theology and the mission of the jesuit college and university. *Conversations*, 5, 5-17.

Heschel, A. (1951). *Man is not alone: A philosophy of religion*. New York: Farrar, Straus and Giroux.

Hodgkinson, V., Weitzman, M., & Kirsch, A. (1988). *From belief to commitment: The activities and finances of religious congregations in the United States*. Washington, DC: Independent Sector.

Hodgkinson, V., Weitzman, M., & Kirsch, A. (1993). *From belief to commitment: The activities and finances of religious congregations in the United States*. Washington, DC: Independent Sector.

James, W. (1990). *The varieties of religious experience*. New York: Vintage Books/The Library of America.

Nolan, A. (1978). *Jesus before christianity*. New York: Orbis Books Maryknoll, 31-33.

Pardeck, J., Murphy, J. & Choi, J. (1994). Some implications of postmodernism for social work practice. *Social Work*, 39, 343-346.

O'Neill, M. (1989). *The third america: The emergence of the nonprofit sector in the United States*. San Francisco: Jossey-Bass, Inc.

The Salvation Army. (1994). *The salvation army 1994 national annual report*. Alexandria, Virginia.

The United Methodist Association of Health and Welfare Ministries. (1988). *A significant ministry: Results of the 1987 survey of health and welfare ministries (adjusted for 1995 estimates)*. Dayton, Ohio.

Weick, K. (1979). *The social psychology of organizing*. Reading, Massachusetts: Addison-Wesley Publishing Company, 134-135.

Advanced Liberalism, (Post)Modernity and Social Work: Some Emerging Social Configurations

Nigel Parton

SUMMARY. The central focus of this paper is to analyze the nature of social work and social welfare in Britain and the Western World more generally. In the process it draws on perspectives in social theory associated with postmodernity, postmodernization and post-Fordism. It argues, however, that such approaches are both too sweeping and more appropriately understood as signifying the nature of current times rather than explaining them. The paper suggests that the current changes are better characterized in terms of advanced liberalism or extended liberal modernity. *[Article copies available for a fee from The Haworth Document Delivery Service: 1-800-342-9678. E-mail address: getinfo@haworth.com]*

Social work at present is living through a period of massive change, which can be characterized as the destabilization of an entire service system (Parton, 1996). As described by Harding (1992) the certitude of a professionally-driven, local authority-controlled service system no longer exists, and few have a clear vision about potential alternatives. At one level these uncertainties arise from the changes ushered in by a variety of social service related

Professor Nigel Parton is affiliated with School of Human and Health Sciences, University of Huddersfield, Queensgate, Huddersfield, HD1 3DH.

[Haworth co-indexing entry note]: "Advanced Liberalism, (Post)Modernity and Social Work: Some Emerging Social Configurations." Parton, Nigel. Co-published simultaneously in *Social Thought* (The Haworth Pastoral Press, an imprint of The Haworth Press, Inc.) Vol. 18, No. 3, 1998, pp. 71-88; and: *Postmodernism, Religion and the Future of Social Work* (ed: Roland G. Meinert, John T. Pardeck, and John W. Murphy) The Haworth Pastoral Press, an imprint of The Haworth Press, Inc., 1998, pp. 71-88. Single or multiple copies of this article are available for a fee from The Haworth Document Delivery Service [1-800-342-9678, 9:00 a.m. - 5:00 p.m. (EST). E-mail address: getinfo@haworth.com].

71

legislation along with changes in the training and education of social workers. At another level, however, they reflect much wider and fundamental changes in the state, the economy, and society more generally. What becomes evident is that the uncertainties that characterize contemporary social work in Britain can also be seen to determine the nature and form of social transformations in Western societies and the United States more generally, in addition to many of the current debates in social theory.

The overall argument of this paper is that western society is currently undergoing changes that are dramatic and transformatory, and which have fundamental impact on the way in which persons think about, prioritize, organize and practice social work and social welfare more generally. However, rather than seeing postmodern perspectives as the most helpful way of explaining or understanding these developments, these frameworks are symptomatic of the current condition. The theoretical and practical claims of postmodernity should be seen largely as a response to the reductionist and reified conceptions of the modern in conventional social science and welfare policy and practice. The particular importance of debates about postmodernity is that they draw attention to key areas of social transformation in terms of: the increasing pace of change; the new complexities and forms of fragmentation; the growing significance of difference, plurality and various emergent political movements and strategies; and the pervasive awareness of relativities, the opening up of individual choice and freedom, and the increasing awareness of the socially constructed nature of reality.

Increasingly, many postmodern interpretations are becoming too sweeping and do not take the situation of actually living human actors sufficiently seriously—human actors who define their lives, consciously act and are constrained from acting, in and by real social contexts. A more adequate analysis needs to get closer to the social transformations of the past twenty to thirty years—of which the discourse on postmodernity is a major part, but more in the realm of the practices of signification, rather than explanation. This paper thus draws on the recent work of Rose (1992; 1993a; 1993b) and Peter Wagner (1992; 1994) in terms of characterizing the current changes in terms of advanced liberalism or extended liberal modernity rather than postmodernity. The current changes should thus be likened in scope and form to the transformations that took place from the end of the nineteenth century onwards, in the move from a restricted liberal modernity to organized modernity or what is usually referred to as the move to welfarism and the emergence of the welfare state.

THE FIRST CRISIS OF MODERNITY: THE EMERGENCE OF SOCIAL WORK

The post-Enlightenment emphasis of a liberal society focused on the idea that human autonomy was in principle universal and without boundaries. In theory, this outlook was truly utopian, but in reality was much more limited and well bounded. In effect, freedom was restricted to an elite group—what Wagner (1994) characterizes as restricted liberal modernity. From a variety of perspectives nineteenth century liberalism was presumed to have failed, and was powerless in the face of the forces of social transformation and individualization of modern society, as evidenced by high rates of suicide, crime and general social disaffection. Economic affairs and the impact of the laissez-faire market had profound social consequences, which had not been alleviated by the early factory legislation. The social and economic changes damaged health, produced danger through the irregularities and vagaries of employment, and encouraged the growth of militant labor and the mob. All these elements fed into the growing concerns about the social question, or as Wagner (1994) calls it—the crisis of restricted liberal modernity—the first crisis of modernity.

During the last quarter of the nineteenth century, political economy gradually relinquished its earlier explicit interlinking of economic and moral laws, and formulated itself as a distinctively economic doctrine, with its own internal laws. At the same time, the domain of civil society became socialized. Statistical investigations revealed gradually the population as a domain with its own specificity and irreducibility. Statistical techniques and sociological investigations revealed the nation to be a set of aggregated statistics with regular fluctuations, and knowable processes with their own laws and cycles (Abrams, 1968). Towns became the target of a variety of interventions—social hygiene, police—which gave rise to further detailed statistical mapping of urban space. As the social body became subjected to new government norms, e.g., registration of births, marriages, deaths, types and number of crimes, new realms of social visibility became the object of investigation by sociologists and social statisticians (Hacking, 1991). A social domain came into being that could be both the object of science–social science– and the territory for a variety of policies–social policies–and interventions.

The emergence of social work is thus associated with the transformations that took place from the mid-nineteenth century onwards around a series of anxieties about the family. Social work provided a personalized strategy to enable government at a distance and was to prove important if the liberal ideal of maintaining autonomous individuals who are at the same time governed was to be realized. This field of inquiry and practice developed as a hybrid in the space, the social (Donzelot, 1979; 1988) between the public and the private spheres and was produced by new relations between the law, administration, medicine, the school and the family. This outcome was seen as a positive solution to a major problem posed for the liberal state. Namely, how can the state establish the health and development of family members who are weak and dependent, particularly children, while promoting the family as the natural sphere for caring for those individuals and thus not intervening in all families (Hirst, 1981)? Originally, in the mid-nineteenth century, this activity was carried out by voluntary philanthropic organizations. Donzelot (1979) argues that two techniques were of significance in their relationship with families, particularly on behalf of children–what he calls moralization and normalization. Moralization involved the use of financial and material assistance, which was used as leverage to encourage poor families to overcome their moral failure. This mode of intervention was used primarily for the deserving poor who could demonstrate that their problems arose for reasons beyond their control. Normalization applied to attempts to spread specific norms of living via education, legislation or health, and involved a response to complaints, invariably from women about men, and hence provided a means of entry into the home. In return for this guidance, and moral and minimal material support, philanthropic workers were given an insight into what was happening inside the home and leverage to bring about changes in behavior and lifestyle.

In the late nineteenth and early twentieth centuries philanthropic activities were increasingly absorbed into the formal institutions of the state. This process continued to the early 1970s, with the introduction of local authority social service departments as the fifth social service (Townsend, 1970). While moralization and normalization were to be the primary forms of contact, this was increasingly framed in legislation that would also provide the possibility for coercive intervention. Tutelage, as Donzelot (1988) calls it, based on the notion of preventive intervention, would combine a number of elements, though coercive intervention would be used for the exceptional circumstances where the techniques or moralization and normalization had failed.

However, the space occupied by social work has always been complex. The ambiguous nature of social work arose from its sphere of operation between civil society, with its allegiances to individuals and families, and the state in the guise of the court and its statutory responsibilities. It occupied the space between the respectable and the dangerous classes, and between those with access to political and speaking rights and those who were excluded (Philp, 1979). In this regard, social work fulfilled an essentially mediating role between those who are actually or potentially excluded and the mainstream of society. In many respects the inherent tensions in social work could be seen to exemplify those at the center of the modern condition, demands of freedom, liberty and democracy on the one hand and the need for discipline and regulation on the other.

THE GROWTH OF SOCIAL WORK IN A PERIOD OF WELFARIST ORGANIZED MODERNITY

The growth and legitimation of social work in the twentieth century was closely allied with the emergence of the welfare state. The central focus of this system of regulation was the classification of the population based on the scientific claims of different experts in the psy complex (Ingleby, 1985; Rose, 1985; 1989). Increasingly modern societies regulated the population by sanctioning the knowledge claims and practices of the new human sciences–particularly medicine, psychiatry, psychology, criminology and social work. The psy complex refers to the network of ideas about the nature of human beings, their perfectibility, the reasons for their behavior and the way they may be classified, selected and controlled. The aim of this complex is to manage and improve individuals by the manipulation of their qualities and attributes, while this practice is dependent on scientific knowledge and professional interventions and expertise. Further, human qualities were seen as measurable and calculable and thereby could be changed, improved, and rehabilitated.

The emergence of modern forms of social regulation was an integral element of the development of the increasingly organized nature of modernity. While human order was recognized to be essentially vulnerable and contingent, through the use of science society could be brought under human control. Contingency was discovered, together with the recognition that things could be regular, repeatable, predictable, and thus ordered. The resulting vision was of a hierarchical harmony reflected in the uncontested and incontestable pronouncements of reason. Where the obsessively legislating, defining, structuring, segregating, classifying, recording universalizing state reflected the splendor of universal and absolute standards of truth (Bauman, 1992). These assumptions were most evident in Britain, and also in the United States, with the establishment of the welfare state. The key aspirations of welfarism lay in the attempts to link the fiscal, calculative, and bureaucratic capabilities of the state apparatus to the regulation of social life (Rose and Miller, 1992). As is often noted, 'Welfarism' in Britain rested on the twin pillars of Keynesianism and Beveridgianism.

The Keynesian element stood for an increase in government involvement to manage economic demand in a market economy through judicious intervention, for example, by increased public expenditure during a recession, especially with the aim of maximizing production and maintaining full employment. The great economic downturn of the inter-war years had demonstrated that left to itself the capitalist market economy could not function properly. The economic and social costs of a laissez-faire approach led to a drastic fall in production and mass unemployment, and political and social unrest was high. The waste and inefficiency of a market economy could be corrected through moderate forms of intervention. Beveridge's notion of insurance was introduced to protect (in its widest sense) against the social hazards of a market economy. Unlike the Keynesian economic position, the social argument for welfarism was not new. Since the days of Bismarck in Germany and Lloyd George in Britain, most capitalist countries had developed forms of social protection underwritten and co-ordinated by the state. What was new in the post second world war period was that the principle of state intervention was made explicit, and the institutional framework that would take responsibility for maintaining minimum standards became a reality. This strategy involved pooling society's resources and spreading the risks. Social insurance fundamentally transformed the mechanisms that integrated the citizen into the social order. Not only were individuals to be protected from the evils of Want, Disease, Idleness, Ignorance and Squalor, but they would be constituted as citizens bound into a system of solidarity and mutual inter-dependence. This approach was considered to be a scientific and statistical method of encouraging passive solidarity among its recipients. Everyone would contribute and everyone would benefit, though some more than others. The overall rationale of welfarism was to make the liberal market society more productive, stable, and harmonious; and the role of government, while more complex and expansive, would be positive and beneficent. A number of assumptions characterize the development of welfarism. The institutional framework of universal social services was seen as the best way of maximizing welfare in modern society, while the state was assumed to work for the whole society and was the best way to foster the common west. Social services were instituted for the benevolent purpose of meeting social needs, compensating socially caused 'diswelfares', and promoting social justice. The underlying functions of these activities were ameliorative, integrative and redistributive. Through increased public expenditure, the cumulative extension of statutory welfare services and the proliferation of government regulations, backed by expert administration, equity, and efficiency, would be guaranteed.

Wagner (1994) calls this phase organized modernity, because it is characterized by the integration of nearly all individuals into comprehensively organized practices. Social mobility existed and was part of the liberties that society offered, but it was the linkage of such liberties with the organization of services that provided the social configuration with the assets that explain its relative stability and tacit consent among most citizens. By the early 1960s, the configuration achieved a certain coherence or closure, so that it appeared to be a natural interlocking order. The Keynesian welfare state in Britain seemed to be operating successfully on a national basis, thereby integrating fully the population through scientific interventions. Not surprisingly, during this period social work and welfarism more generally were imbued with a degree of optimism, which assumed that measured and significant improvements could be made in the lives of individuals and families via judicious professional theories, models, and practices.

THE RECONSTRUCTION OF SOCIAL WORK AND SOCIAL WELFARE

However, at the point when modern social work emerged in the early 1970s to play a significant part in the welfarist project of organized modernity, welfarism was experiencing considerable strains and ultimately crises. A combination of slow economic growth, increases in inflation, a growth in social disorder, and a lack of discipline undermined the central economic and social pillars of welfarism and the political consensus that supported this policy. At one level the criticisms leveled at social work from the mid-1970s can be understood as a specific case of the neo-liberal or new right approach, which has dominated government in recent years in terms of: an antagonism towards public expenditure on state welfare; an increasing emphasis on self-help and family support; the centrality of individual responsibility, choice and freedom; and an extension of the commodification of social relations. However, this conclusion would be simplistic. Vocal criticism has come from a variety of quarters, including the left, feminists and anti-racists, a variety of user groups, other professional and community interests, as well as the anti-welfarist right (Clarke, 1993). Increasingly social work and, in particular, social service departments were seen as costly, ineffective, distant, and oppressive.

What has emerged is a reconstruction of social work and the agencies where it operates, which is very consistent with the central themes that characterize the reconstruction of welfare more generally. First, a particular emphasis is placed on market principles primarily through the quasi-market (Le Grand, 1990; Le Grand and Bartlett, 1993) that has a number of features: a split between purchasing and providing responsibilities; a concern for services to be based on need and the assessment of risk rather than historic demand and service levels; the delegation of authority for budgetary control; and the pursuit of choice through provider competition. Second, government by contract (Stewart, 1993) has emerged. The introduction of contractual rather than hierarchical accountability, whereby relationships within and between welfare organizations should be specific and formally outlined and costed. Similarly, at the consumer/professional interface, the nature of the relationships and the focus of work should be formally spelled out in a contract. And third, the development of more responsive and often flatter organizations is encouraged, where responsibilities and decisions are devolved down and where the user/consumer is more directly involved. Notions such as enabling, decentralization, and empowerment are seen as of significance, along with changes in the meaning of professionalism. Various performance indicators, outcome measures, and business plans are introduced.

In this process, the role and practices of managers become crucial. Managers, as opposed to professionals, are the key brokers in the new network (Clarke, Cochrane and McLaughlin, 1994; Cutler and Waine, 1994). Specifically, notions of management frame and supplant the central activities of the professionals and the forms of knowledge they draw on. There is a clear move away from approaches to social work that are based on therapeutic models and which stress the significance of casework. Social workers, reconstituted as casemanagers, are required to act as co-ordinators of care packages for individuals on the basis of an assessment of need or risk. And casemanagers crucially require: skills in the assessment of need and/or risk; co-ordinating packages of care; costing and managing the budgets for services; and monitoring and evaluating progress and outcome.

The emergence of child protection, as a central activity for social workers, underlines the centrality of social workers in providing social assessments of individual risk and 'dangerousness' (Parton, Thorpe and Wattam, 1996), but which recognizes there are various interests and rights at stake–particularly those of the child and parent(s). Decisions in child welfare are now carried out in a more legalized context, where the need for forensic evidence is a priority. The individualized assessment and management of risk, and separating the high risk from the rest, becomes crucial so that both harm to children and unwarrantable interventions in the family can be avoided. Similarly, it is recognized that people have diverse interests and that situations and risks may be judged differently in different circumstances and according to different criteria, e.g., arising from different class or ethnic backgrounds the monolithic notions of knowledge and power are questioned. Especially recognized is that cultural relativities are important and that professionals may not always be the best providers of services.

Therefore, a complex reconstitution of generic social work, and the unified model of the personal social services can be identified. A number of elements are evident. First, increased specialization around client groups, and the separation of assessment and care management from the work of direct service provision is emphasized. Second, the concentration of professionally qualified staff in certain roles and responsibilities is most important–again around assessment and casemanagement–while an increasing number of services are provided by unqualified staff. Third, these changes attempt to shift the power relationship between the client–now consumer or service user–and the professional. Clearly notions of management become central. No longer are social workers constituted as caseworkers, drawing on their therapeutic skills in human relationships, but as casemanagers who assess need and risk and operationalize packages of care in an individualized way.

THE NATURE OF THE EMERGING
SOCIAL CONFIGURATION

Social work appears to be increasing in diversity, uncertainty, fragmentation, and ambiguity–all themes that have been the focus of attention in social theory, and are considered to be indicative of the emergence of the postmodern. Recent years have witnessed an increasing interest in understanding changes in welfare in terms of postmodernity (see Williams, 1992; Burrows and Loader, 1994; and Taylor-Gooby, 1994), and some writers have applied such approaches to social work in particular (see Rojek, Peacock and Collins, 1988; McBeath and Webb, 1991; Sands and Nuccio, 1992; Pardeck, Murphy and Chung, 1994; Parton, 1994a; Parton, 1994b; Pozatek, 1994; Howe, 1994). Some critics argue that these changes have been overstated or over signified (Clarke, 1991); others claim that the changes, at the economic and political level, merely represent new forms of class relations in the pursuit of profit and exploitation (Callinicos, 1989; Jameson, 1991); and others write that these transformations do not represent a distinct break with the past but a period of late or high modernity (Giddens, 1990, 1991). Nonetheless, something significant appears to be occurring.

Notions of postmodernity, postmodernization, and post-Fordism serve to describe the central features and processes of the various global transformations taking place since the early 1960s. For while production has been the key influence on modern society–the way it is organized for production considerably influences the political, cultural and social spheres–this is no longer necessarily the case. Postmodernization involves a reversal of determinacy, so that the fragments of a hyper differentiating culture disrupt and deconstruct areas of social structure that were previously treated as central and immovable–particularly social class. For example, there is a massive compression of time and space, particularly via the pervasive impact of information technology and the growth of media (Harvey, 1989). Markets become saturated and consumers begin to exercise choice, while production systems are forced into structural changes that allow flexible responses to new and different consumer demands (Crook, Pakulski and Waters, 1992). The growth of new technology allows for a number of changes in the organization of work in contemporary society: the service sector is expanded by the reduction of labor required for production; the reduction of capital costs of production increases the possibilities for self-employment; and new opportunities are opened up for alternative forms of organization that do not rely on hierarchy, bureaucracy, and the traditional professional and occupational roles. Notions of flexibility and fragmentation, in both production and organization, are increasingly evident, which are referred to as flexible accumulation or post-Fordism.

Suggested is that if Fordism is represented by notions of mass production, mass consumption, modernist cultural forms, and the mass public provision of welfare, then post-Fordism is characterized by an emerging coalition between flexible production, differentiated and segmented consumption patterns, post-modern cultural forms, and a restructured welfare state (Loader and Burrows, 1994). Williams (1994) has argued that at an elementary level applying post-Fordist analysis to welfare suggests that changes in the design of both production and consumption in the larger economy have influenced and even been reproduced within the delivery of social services in: mass production to flexible production; mass consumption to diverse patterns of consumption; production-led to consumer-led; from mass, universal needs met by monolithic, bureaucratic/professional-led provision to the diversity of individual needs met by welfare pluralism, quasi-markets, reorganized welfare work and consumer sovereignty. Central to these changes are moves to create the flexible organization of different work patterns, lines of accountability, and forms of decision-making. The emphasis is on strategic management, quality control processes, responsiveness, creativity, teamwork, managerial decentralization, flexibility of labor, and numerical flexibility. A key element in this complex and diverse reconceptualization and restructuring of state welfare is a new role for management. In recent years, the growth of managerialism has been the thread linking markets, partnerships, an emphasis on customers, and the recomposition of the labor force (Taylor-Gooby and Lawson, 1993). This shift is transforming the relationships of power, culture, control, and accountability (Clarke, Cochrane and McLaughlin, 1994).

The development of flexible organizations and new technology allows for the transfer of productive capacity, or service provision, out of the core organizations. A variety of consequences result from this reorientation. Permanent full-time workers in the core organization need new training, as their personal skills and abilities assume increasing importance; middle management is released and specialized services are contracted out on a need basis; labor intensive production (or service provision) requiring high levels of supervision is externalized; and in many instances the process of decentralization goes so far as to deconstruct the core organization into a looser arrangement. Around core organizations are emerging networks of smaller-scale units, with a variety of contractual arrangements between organizations and their own employees. These include: small professional and technical organizations operate on a fee-for or consultancy service with a pronounced petty entrepreneurial character; specialist craft workshops produce niche-market products or complex services supplied to core organizations on a contractual basis; labor-intensive sweat-shops employ the secondary labor market on a frequent basis; entrepreneurial contract suppliers, in various manual services such as cleansing and catering, take advantage of the secondary labor market; and most workers are subject to increasing insecurity and little material reward.

The notion of postmodernity recognizes that persons now inhabit a world that has become disorientated, disturbed, and subject to doubt. The pursuit of order and control, the promotion of calculability, the belief in progress, science and rationality, and other features intrinsic to modernity are increasingly being undermined by a simultaneous range of negative conditions and experiences and the persistence of chance and the threat of indeterminacy. Postmodernity is characterized as the fragmentation of modernity into forms of institutional pluralism, marked by variety, difference, contingency, relativism and ambivalence–all of which modernity sought to overcome. A constant and growing questioning of modern resolutions has been diagnosed as symptomatic of the postmodern condition, particularly the expansion of reason and quick technological fixes to social problems.

Even those who are highly critical of claims that society is moving towards the postmodern recognize that the average person is experiencing a considerable loss of confidence in science and experts providing solutions to economic, social, and human problems (Taylor-Gooby, 1994). Increasingly notions of ambivalence, contingency, risk and reflexivity are seen as characteristic of the contemporary condition. Thus, a central postmodern tenet is the refusal to prescribe some discourses as essentially true, and to proscribe others as irredeemably false. For a key postmodern operation is that of deconstruction, whereby phenomena are continually interrogated, evaluated, disrupted, and overturned. Nothing is taken for granted, and phenomena are always likely to be subject to critique and changed. Postmodernists pluralize and politicize the processes of reaching a verdict in areas which were previously taken for granted and closed off, thereby politicizing all areas of personal and social life.

CONCLUSIONS: COMPARING THE AMERICAN EXPERIENCE

However, as intimated at the outset, these transformations should not necessarily be characterized as postmodern. While it is perhaps premature to finalize the nature of the emergent social reconfigurations, following the second crisis of modernity in recent years, there is a danger in seeing the breaks with the past as too clear cut. In many respects, these changes should be viewed to be the result of the inherent tensions of modernity, in terms of liberty and discipline, but which were submerged and closed off during the period of organized modernity. Most troublesome is that the elements and characteristics of what Wagner (1994) calls organized modernity are passed off as modernity more generally, thus encouraging the present to be viewed as postmodern. In part, this argument becomes more convincing by reflecting on parallel changes in the USA. In many respects the United States has never had an equivalent of the British, or Western European, welfare state. This history stemmed, in part, from the impossibility of defining obligations with regard to national citizenship. An analysis of the more open, boundless American experience highlights the particular character of organized modernity in Europe. Key aspects of nineteenth-century Europe that contributed to the first crisis of modernity, and which were central to the emergence of organized modernity, were virtually absent in the United States. The United States has had minimal experience with a centralized state, has had fewer restrictions on political participation, no homogeneous cultural-linguistic identity, and no explicit social question. While society has been dominated by white, Anglo-Saxon, and (various) Christian sections of the population, the United States is far too plurally composed for any common ethnic or religious identity to emerge. In sum, after its revolution in the late eighteenth century, the United States built a less restricted, more individualized and more liberal modernity than Britain and the other European countries.

In many respects, the deficiencies of postmodern political perspectives and hence their implications for social welfare, mark the major problematics of social organization in the United States. While invariably seeing themselves on the political left, postmodern discourses seem to provide simply a mirror to an increasingly fragmented and segregated society. They have great difficulty in suggesting how things can be improved and how improvements might be judged. There is an almost complete neglect of political deliberation about common, social matters. Postmodernists' major strength is their recognition of plurality, diversity and relativities—and by implication the support of suppressed groups—but they have difficulty in developing arguments or practices at the level of the polity and everyday affairs.

The key point at this juncture is that at the core of the modern project is an inherent tension between liberty and discipline, and that while, in Britain and Europe, this was partially resolved or closed off for many years under the conditions of organized modernity, this is no longer the case. Issues of choice, freedom, and individual social construction have again come to the fore in ways that have been far more evident in the United States. These tensions and ambiguities, additionally, lie at the core of social work. There should be no surprise, therefore, that the purpose of social work is increasingly uncertain and subject to critiques from various quarters. Nor perhaps is it surprising that practice is taking place in an increasingly hostile environment, where an increased incidence of poverty and the underclass is evident (Morris, 1994). In many respects, the experiences of social work in the United Kingdom, and elsewhere in Europe, are increasingly reflecting those in the United States. However, rather than characterize these changes in terms of the postmodern, they should be viewed as an example of extended liberal modernity (Wagner, 1994) or advanced liberalism (Rose, 1993). Accordingly, the tensions and ambiguities of the modern project, in terms of liberty and discipline, also lie at the core of social work and capture its essential nature for both practitioners and those who receive services. While these tensions were submerged during organized modernity, they have returned in contemporary social transformations, although their full implications have not been realized.

REFERENCES

Abrams, P. (1968). *The Origins of British Sociology 1834-1914*. Chicago, University of Chicago Press.

Bauman, Z. (1992). *Intimations of Postmodernity*. London, Routledge.

Burrows, R. and Loader, B. (eds) (1994). *Towards a Post-Fordist Welfare State?* London, Routledge.

Callinicos, A. (1989). *Against Postmodernism: A Marxist Critique*. Cambridge, Polity Press.

Clarke, J. (1991). *New Times and Old Enemies: Essays on Cultural Studies and America*. London, Harper Collins.

Clarke, J. (ed) (1993). *A Crisis in Care? Challenges to Social Work*. London, Sage.

Clarke, J., Cochrane, A. and McLaughlin, E. (eds) (1994). *Managing Social Policy*. London, Sage.

Crook, S., Pakulski, J. and Waters, M. (1992). *Postmodernization: Change in Advanced Society*. London, Sage.

Cutler, T. and Waine, B. (1994). *Managing the Welfare State: The Politics of Public Sector Management*. Oxford, Berg.

Donzelot, J. (1979). *The Policing of Families*. London, Hutchinson.

Donzelot, J. (1988). *The Promotion of the Social, Economy and Society*, 17, pp. 395-427.

Giddens, A. (1990). *The Consequences of Modernity*. Cambridge, Polity Press.

Giddens, A. (1991). *Modernity and Self-Identity: Self and Society in the Late Modern Age*. Cambridge, Polity Press.

Hacking, I. (1991). *How should we do the history of statistics?* in G. Burchell, C. Gordon and P. Miller (eds) *The Foucault Effect: Studies in Governmentality*. London, Harvester-Wheatsheaf.

Harding, T. (1992). Questions on the social services agenda, in T. Harding (ed) *Who Owns Welfare? Questions on the Social Services Agenda. Social Services Policy Forum Paper II*. London, National Institute for Social Work.

Harvey, D. (1989). *The Condition of Postmodernity: An Enquiry into the Origins of Cultural Change*. Oxford, Blackwell.

Hirst, P. (1981). The Genesis of the Social. *Politics and Power*, 3, pp. 67-82.

Howe, D. (1994). Modernity, Postmodernity and Social Work. *British Journal of Social Work*, 24, pp. 513-532.

Ingleby, D. (1985). Professionals as socializers: The psy complex, in A. Scully and S. Spitzer (eds). *Research in Law, Deviance and Social Control 7*. New York, Jai Press.

Jameson, F. (1991). *Postmodernism or the Cultural Logic of Late Capitalism.* London, Verso.

Le Grand, J. (1990). *Quasi-Markets and Social Policy.* School for Advanced Urban Studies, University of Bristol.

Le Grand, J. and Bartlett, W. (1993). *Quasi-Markets and Social Policy.* Basingstoke, Macmillan.

McBeath, G.B. and Webb, S.A. (1991). Social Work, Modernity and Postmodernity, *Sociological Review,* 39, 4, pp. 171-192.

Morris, L. (1994). *Dangerous Classes: The Underclass and Social Citizenship.* London, Routledge.

Pardeck, J.T., Murphy, J.W. and Chung, W.S. (1994). Social Work and Postmodernism. *Social Work and Social Science Review,* 5, pp. 113-123.

Parton, N. (1994a). Problematics of Government, (Post)Modernity and Social Work. *British Journal of Social Work,* 24, pp. 9-32.

Parton, N. (1994b). Social Work under conditions of (Post)Modernity. *Social Work and Social Science Review,* 5, pp. 93-112.

Parton, N. (1996). *Social Theory, Social Change and Social Work.* London, Routledge.

Parton, N., Thorpe, D. and Wattam, C. (1996). *Child Protection: Risk and the Moral Order.* London, Macmillan.

Philp, M. (1979). Notes on the Form of Knowledge in Social Work. *Sociological Review,* 27, pp. 83-111.

Pozatek, E. (1994). The Problem of Certainty: Clinical Social Work in the Postmodern Era. *Social Work,* 39, pp. 396-403.

Rojek, C., Peacock, G. and Collins, S. (1988). *Social Work and Received Ideas.* London, Routledge.

Rose, N. (1985). *The Psychological Complex: Psychology, Politics and Society in England, 1869-1939.* London, Routledge, Kegan Paul.

Rose, N. (1989). *Governing the Soul: The shaping of the private self.* London, Routledge.

Rose, N. (1993a). Government, authority and expertise in advanced liberalism. *Economy and Society,* 22, pp. 283-299.

Rose, N. (1993b). Disadvantage and power after the Welfare State, Finnish translation, *Janus (Journal of the Finnish Society for Social Policy),* 1, pp. 44-68.

Rose, N. and Miller, P. (1992). Political power beyond the State: Problematics of government. *British Journal of Sociology,* 43, pp. 173-205.

Sands, R.G. and Nuccio, K. (1992). Postmodern Feminist Theory and Social Work. *Social Work,* 37, pp. 489-494.

Stewart, J. (1993). The limitations of government by contract. *Public Money and Management,* July/September, pp. 7-12.

Taylor-Gooby, P. (1994). Postmodernism and Social Policy: A Great Leap Backwards? *Journal of Social Policy,* 23, pp. 385-404.

Taylor-Gooby, P. and Lawson, R. (eds) (1993). *Markets and Managers: New Issues in the Delivery of Welfare.* Milton Keynes, Open University Press.

Townsend, P. (ed) (1970). *The Fifth Social Service: A Critical Analysis of the Seebohm Proposals*. London, The Fabian Society.

Wagner, P. (1992). Liberty and discipline: Making sense of postmodernity, or, once again, towards a sociohistorical understanding of modernity. *Theory and Society*, 22, pp. 467-92.

Wagner, P. (1994). *A Sociology of Modernity: Liberty and Discipline*. London, Routledge.

Williams, F. (1992). Somewhere over the rainbow: universality and diversity in social policy, in *Social Policy Review*, 4, pp. 200-219.

Williams, F. (1994). Social relations, welfare and the post-Fordist debate, in R. Burrows and B. Loader (eds) *Towards a Post-Fordist Welfare State*. London, Sage.

Index

Haworth
DOCUMENT DELIVERY
SERVICE

This valuable service provides a single-article order form for any article from a Haworth journal.

- *Time Saving:* No running around from library to library to find a specific article.
- *Cost Effective:* All costs are kept down to a minimum.
- *Fast Delivery:* Choose from several options, including same-day FAX.
- *No Copyright Hassles:* You will be supplied by the original publisher.
- *Easy Payment:* Choose from several easy payment methods.

Open Accounts Welcome for ...
- Library Interlibrary Loan Departments
- Library Network/Consortia Wishing to Provide Single-Article Services
- Indexing/Abstracting Services with Single Article Provision Services
- Document Provision Brokers and Freelance Information Service Providers

---

MAIL or *FAX* THIS ENTIRE ORDER FORM TO:

Haworth Document Delivery Service
The Haworth Press, Inc.
10 Alice Street
Binghamton, NY 13904-1580

or FAX: 1-800-895-0582
or CALL: 1-800-342-9678
9am-5pm EST

PLEASE SEND ME PHOTOCOPIES OF THE FOLLOWING SINGLE ARTICLES:

1) Journal Title: _____
   Vol/Issue/Year:_____Starting & Ending Pages:_____
   Article Title:_____

2) Journal Title: _____
   Vol/Issue/Year:_____Starting & Ending Pages:_____
   Article Title:_____

3) Journal Title: _____
   Vol/Issue/Year:_____Starting & Ending Pages:_____
   Article Title:_____

4) Journal Title: _____
   Vol/Issue/Year:_____Starting & Ending Pages:_____
   Article Title:_____

(See other side for Costs and Payment Information)

COSTS: Please figure your cost to order quality copies of an article.

1. Set-up charge per article: $8.00
   ($8.00 × number of separate articles) _____

2. Photocopying charge for each article:

   1-10 pages: $1.00 _____

   11-19 pages: $3.00 _____

   20-29 pages: $5.00 _____

   30+ pages: $2.00/10 pages _____

3. Flexicover (optional): $2.00/article _____

4. Postage & Handling: US: $1.00 for the first article/

   $.50 each additional article _____

   Federal Express: $25.00 _____

   Outside US: $2.00 for first article/

   $.50 each additional article _____

5. Same-day FAX service: $.35 per page _____

                                        GRAND TOTAL: _____

METHOD OF PAYMENT: (please check one)

❏ Check enclosed   ❏ Please ship and bill. PO # _____
                     (sorry we can ship and bill to bookstores only! All others must pre-pay)

❏ Charge to my credit card: ❏ Visa; ❏ MasterCard; ❏ Discover;
                             ❏ American Express;

Account Number: _____ Expiration date: _____

Signature: *X* _____

Name: _____ Institution: _____

Address: _____

_____

City: _____ State: _____ Zip: _____

Phone Number: _____ FAX Number: _____

MAIL or *FAX* THIS ENTIRE ORDER FORM TO:

Haworth Document Delivery Service	**or FAX:** 1-800-895-0582
The Haworth Press, Inc.	**or CALL:** 1-800-342-9678
10 Alice Street	9am-5pm EST)
Binghamton, NY 13904-1580	

FORTHCOMING and NEW BOOKS IN RELIGION, MINISTRY & PASTORAL CARE

THE PASTOR'S FAMILY

NEW!

The Challenges of Family Life and Pastoral Responsibilities
Daniel L. Langford, DMin, MSW
Brings to the attention of ministers, churches, and policymakers of Christian organizations the often mute suffering and neglect experienced by ministers' wives and children.
$29.95 hard. ISBN: 0-7890-0584-0.
ISBN: 0-7890-0585-9.
Available Fall 1998. Approx. 126 pp. with Index.
Features photographs and many personal reflections and stories.

WHAT THE DYING TEACH US

NEW!

Lessons on Living
Reverend Samuel Lee Oliver, BCC
A collection of actual experiences and insights shared by terminally ill persons.
$29.95 hard. ISBN: 0-7890-0475-5.
$14.95 soft. ISBN: 0-7890-0476-3.
Available Summer 1998. Approx. 114 pp. with Index.
Features personal reflections on death and dying.

SPIRITUAL CRISIS

NEW!

Surviving Trauma to the Soul
J. LeBron McBride, PhD
Discover how you can reverse the impact of spiritual crisis and apply healing balm to the traumatized soul.
$39.95 hard. ISBN: 0-7890-0135-7.
$19.95 soft. ISBN: 0-7890-0460-7.
1998. Available now. 207 pp. with Index.
Features case studies, tables, and figures.

HIDDEN ADDICTIONS

NEW!

A Pastoral Response to the Abuse of Legal Drugs
Bridget Clare McKeever, PhD, SSL
Shows you the social roots of addiction and gives you the spiritual and religious resources necessary to put you and your loved ones on the road to holistic recovery.
$29.95 hard. ISBN: 0-7890-0266-3.
$14.95 soft. ISBN: 0-7890-0267-1.
1998. Available now. 197 pp. with Index.
Features case studies and a bibliography.

UNDERSTANDING CLERGY MISCONDUCT IN RELIGIOUS SYSTEMS

NEW!

Scapegoating, Family Secrets, and the Abuse of Power
Candace R. Benyei, PhD
Helps you see leaders of religious institutions in a way that the world has been afraid to see them—in a glass clearly.
$29.95 hard. ISBN: 0-7890-0451-8.
$19.95 soft. ISBN: 0-7890-0452-6.
1998. Available now. 197 pp. with Index.
Features a glossary and appendixes.

THE EIGHT MASKS OF MEN

NEW!

A Practical Guide in Spiritual Growth for Men of the Christian Faith
Rev. Dr. Frederick G. Grosse
This book will encourage you to come out from behind your mask of solitude and loneliness—one of man's most obtrusive masks—and reach out for help and community.
$39.95 hard. ISBN: 0-7890-0415-1.
$19.95 soft. ISBN: 0-7890-0416-X.1997. 154 pp. with Index.
Features anecdotal stories and excerpts by men who have undergone spiritual group work and an appendix of biblical references for spiritual growth.

WHEN LIFE MEETS DEATH

NEW!

Stories of Death and Dying, Truth and Courage
Thomas William Shane, DDiv
A book of stories from people who have faced the ordinary, yet overwhelming, experience of the death of a loved one.
$24.95 hard. ISBN: 0-7890-0289-2.1997. 146 pp. with Index.

THE HEART OF PASTORAL COUNSELING

Healing Through Relationship, Revised Edition
Richard Dayringer, ThD
NEW!
On the first edition:
"A comprehensive volume that offers concrete help and provides ladders for those suffering counseling pitfalls."
—Ministry
$39.95 hard. ISBN: 0-7890-0172-1
$19.95 soft. ISBN: 0-7890-0421-6.
1998. Available now. 205 pp. with Index.
Features 4 appendixes, charts/figures, diagnostic criteria, and a bibliography.

DYING, GRIEVING, FAITH, AND FAMILY

A Pastoral Care Approach
George W. Bowman, III, ThM, BD
NEW!
Provocative, suggestive, and stimulating to professionals and educators working with and teaching about dying and grieving persons.
$39.95 hard. ISBN: 0-7890-0262-0.
$19.95 soft. ISBN: 0-7890-0263-9. 1997. 150 pp. with Index.

THE PASTORAL CARE OF DEPRESSION

A Guidebook
Binford W. Gilbert, PhD
NEW!
Shows pastors how to help people who come to them in a state of depression.
$29.95 hard. ISBN: 0-7890-0264-7.
$14.95 soft. ISBN: 0-7890-0265-5. 1997. 127 pp. with Index.

Faculty: Textbooks are available for classroom adoption consideration on a 60-day examination basis. You will receive an invoice payable within 60 days along with the book. If you decide to adopt the book, your invoice will be cancelled. Please write to us on your institutional letterhead, indicating the textbook you would like to examine as well as the following information: course title, current text, enrollment, and decision date.

The Haworth Pastoral Press
An imprint of the The Haworth Press, Inc.
10 Alice Street
Binghamton, New York 13904–1580 USA

Visit our online catalog and search for publications of interest to you by title, author, keyword, or subject!
http://www.haworthpressinc.com

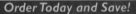